The Ocean of Theosophy

The
Ocean of Theosophy

William Q. Judge

THEOSOPHICAL UNIVERSITY PRESS
PASADENA, CALIFORNIA

Theosophical University Press
Post Office Box C
Pasadena, California 91109–7107
www.theosociety.org
2002

The text of this edition is verbatim with the 1893 Second Edition revised by William Q. Judge. It has been reset in larger type with quotations and typographical errors corrected.

∞

The paper in this book is recycled and meets the standards for permanence and durability of the Council on Library Resources.

Library of Congress Information

LC Control Number: 73078147
Author: Judge, William Quan (1851–1896)
Title: The Ocean of Theosophy
Description: xiii, 173, xx p.; 21 cm.
ISBN 0-911500-25-1 (cloth : alk. paper)
ISBN 0-911500-26-x (pbk. : alk. paper)
Notes: First published in 1893.
Includes index.
Subjects: Theosophy
LC Classification: BP565.J82 1973
Dewey Class No.: 212/.52

Manufactured in the United States of America

PREFACE

AN attempt is made in the pages of this book to write of theosophy in such a manner as to be understood by the ordinary reader. Bold statements are made in it upon the knowledge of the writer, but at the same time it is distinctly to be understood that he alone is responsible for what is therein written: the Theosophical Society is not involved in nor bound by anything said in the book, nor are any of its members any the less good Theosophists because they may not accept what I have set down. The tone of settled conviction which may be thought to pervade the chapters is not the result of dogmatism or conceit, but flows from knowledge based upon evidence and experience.

Members of the Theosophical Society will notice that certain theories or doctrines have not been gone into. That is because they could not be treated without unduly extending the book and arousing needless controversy.

The subject of the Will has received no treatment, inasmuch as that power or faculty is hidden, subtle, undiscoverable as to essence, and only visible in effect. As it is absolutely colorless and varies in moral quality in accordance with the desire behind it, as also it acts frequently without our knowledge, and as it operates in all the kingdoms below man, there could be nothing gained by attempting to enquire into it apart from the Spirit and the desire.

I claim no originality for this book. I invented none of it, discovered none of it, but have simply written that which I have been taught and which has been proved to me. It therefore is only a handing on of what has been known before.

WILLIAM Q. JUDGE

New York, May, 1893.

CONTENTS

CHAPTER I

THEOSOPHY AND THE MASTERS

Theosophy generally defined. The existence of highly developed men in the Universe. These men are the Mahatmas, Initiates, Brothers, Adepts. How they work and why they remain now concealed. Their Lodge. They are perfected men from other periods of evolution. They have had various names in history. Apollonius, Moses, Solomon, and others were members of this fraternity. They had one single doctrine. They are possible because man may at last be as they are. They keep the true doctrine and cause it to reappear at the right time. Pages 1 to 14.

CHAPTER II

GENERAL PRINCIPLES

A view of the general laws governing the Cosmos. The sevenfold division in the system. Real Matter not visible and this always known to the Lodge. Mind the intelligent portion of the Cosmos. In the universal Mind the sevenfold plan of the Cosmos is contained. Evolution proceeds upon the plan in the universal Mind. Periods of Evolution come to an end; this is the Night of Brahma. The Mosaic account of Cosmogenesis has dwarfed modern conceptions. The Jews had merely one part of the doctrine taken from the ancient Egyptians. The doctrine accords with the inner meaning of Genesis. The general length of periods of Evolution. Same doctrine as Herbert Spencer's. The old Hindu chronology gives the details. The story of Solomon's Temple is that of the evolution of man. The doctrine far older than the Christian one. The real age of the world. Man is over 18,000,000 years old. Evolution is accomplished solely by the Egos within that at last become the users of human forms. Each of the seven principles of man is derived from one of the seven great divisions of the Universe. Pages 15 to 24.

CHAPTER III

THE EARTH CHAIN

The doctrine respecting the Earth. It is sevenfold also. It is one of a chain of seven corresponding to man. The whole seven are not in a chain separated as to members, but they interpenetrate each other. The Earth chain is the reincarnation of a former old and now dead chain. This old chain was one of which our moon is the visible representative. Moon now dead and contracting. Venus, Mars, etc., are living members of other similar chains to ours. A mass of Egos for each chain. The number, though incalculable, is definite. Their course of evolution through the seven globes. In each a certain part of our nature is developed. At the fourth globe the process of condensation is begun and reaches its limit. Pages 25 to 31.

CHAPTER IV

SEPTENARY CONSTITUTION OF MAN

The constitution of man. How the doctrine differs from the ordinary Christian one. The real doctrine known in the first centuries of this era, but purposely withdrawn from a nation not able to bear it. The danger if the doctrine had not been withdrawn. The sevenfold division. The principles classified. The divisions agree with the chain of seven globes. The lower man is a composite being. His higher trinity. The lower four principles transitory and perishable. Death leaves the trinity as the only persistent part of us. What the physical man is, and what the other unseen mortal man is. A second physical man not seen but still mortal. The senses pertain to the unseen man and not to the visible one.

Pages 32 to 38.

CHAPTER V

BODY AND ASTRAL BODY

The body and life principle. The mystery of life. Sleep and death are due to excess of life not bearable by the organism. The body an illusion. What is the cell. Life is universal. It is not the result of the organism. The Astral Body. What it is made of. Its powers and functions. As a model for the body. It is possessed by all kingdoms of nature. Its power to travel. The real sense organs are in the astral body. The place the astral body has at spiritualistic *séances*. The astral body accounts for telepathy, clairvoyance, clairaudience, and all such psychical phenomena. Pages 39 to 50.

CHAPTER VI

KAMA — DESIRE

The fourth principle. Kama Rupa. In English, the Passions and Desires. Kama Rupa is not produced by the body but is the cause for body. This is the balance principle of the seven. It is the basis of action and mover of the will. Right desire leads to right act. This principle has a higher and a lower aspect. The principle is in the astral body. At death it coalesces with the astral body and makes of it a shell of the man. It has powers of its own of an automatic nature. This shell is the so-called "spirit" of *séances*. It is a danger to the race. Elementals help this shell at *séances*. No soul or conscience present. Suicides and executed criminals leave very coherent shells. The principle of desire is common to all the organized kingdoms. It is the brute part of man. Man is now a fully developed quaternary with the higher principles partially developed. Pages 51 to 58.

CHAPTER VII

MANAS

Manas the fifth principle. The first of the real man. This is the thinking principle and is not the product of brain. Brain is only its instrument. How the light of mind was given to mindless men. Perfected men from older systems gave it to us as they got it from their predecessors. Manas is the storehouse of all thoughts. Manas is the seer. If the connection between Manas and brain is broken the person is not able to cognize. The organs of the body cognize nothing. Manas is divided into upper and lower. Its four peculiarities. Buddha, Jesus, and others had Manas fully developed. Atma the Divine Ego. The permanent individuality. This permanent individuality has been through every sort of experience in many bodies. Manas and matter have now a greater facility of action than in former times. Manas is bound by desire, and this makes reincarnation a necessity. Pages 59 to 67.

CHAPTER VIII

OF REINCARNATION

Why is man as he is, and how did he come. What the Universe is for. Spiritual and physical evolution demand reincarnation. Reincarnation on the physical plane is reembodiment or alteration of form. The whole mass of matter of the globe will one day be men in a period far distant. The doctrine ancient. Held by the early Christians. Taught by Jesus. What reincarnates. Life's mysteries arise from incomplete incarnation of the higher principles. It is not transmigration to lower forms. Explanation of Manu on this. Pages 68 to 78.

CHAPTER IX

REINCARNATION CONTINUED

Objections urged. Desire cannot alter law. Early arrivals in heaven. Must they wait for us. Recognition of the soul not dependent on objectivity. Heredity not an objection. What heredity does. Divergences in heredity not recognized. History goes against heredity. Reincarnation not unjust. What is justice. We do not suffer for another's but for our own deeds. Memory. Why we do not remember other lives. Who does? How to account for increase of population. Pages 79 to 88.

CHAPTER X

ARGUMENTS SUPPORTING REINCARNATION

From the nature of the soul. From the laws of mind and soul. From differences in character. From the necessity for discipline and evolution. From differences of capacity and start in life at the cradle. Individual identity proves it. The probable object of life makes it necessary. One life not enough to carry out Nature's purposes. Mere death confers no advance. A school after death is illogical. The persistence of savagery and the decay of nations give support to it. The appearance of geniuses is due to reincarnation. Inherent ideas common to man show it. Opposition to the doctrine based solely on prejudice. Pages 89 to 99.

CHAPTER XI

KARMA

Definition of the word. An unfamiliar term. A beneficent law. How present life is affected by past acts of other lives. Each act has a thought at its root. Through Manas they react on each personal life. Why people are born deformed or in bad circumstances. The three classes of Karma and its three fields of operation. National and Racial Karma. Individual unhappiness and happiness. The Master's words on Karma. Pages 100 to 111.

CHAPTER XII

KAMA LOKA

The first state after death. Where and what are heaven and hell? Death of the body only the first step of death. A second death after that. Separation of the seven principles into three classes. What is *Kama Loka*? Origin of Christian purgatory. It is an astral sphere with numerous degrees. The *Skandhas*. The astral shell of man in *Kama Loka*. It is devoid of soul, mind, and conscience. It is the "spirit" of the *séance* rooms. Classification of shells in *Kama Loka*. Black magicians there. Fate of suicides and others. Pre-devachanic unconsciousness. Pages 112 to 122.

Manas - storehouse of all thought

CHAPTER XIII

DEVACHAN

The meaning of the term. A state of *Atma-Buddhi-Manas.* Operation of Karma on Devachan. The necessity for Devachan. It is another sort of thinking with no physical body to clog it. Only two fields for operation of causes — subjective and objective. Devachan is one. No time there for the soul. Length of stay therein. Mathematics of the soul. Average stay therein is 1500 mortal years. Depends on psychic impulses of life. Its use and purpose. On the last thoughts at death the devachanic state is fashioned. Devachan not meaningless. Do we see those left behind? We bring their images before us. Entities in Devachan have a power to help those they love. Mediums cannot go to those in Devachan except in rare cases and when the person is pure. Adepts only can help those in Devachan. Pages 123 to 131.

CHAPTER XIV

CYCLES

One of the most important doctrines. Corresponding words in the Sanskrit. Few cycles known to the West. They cause the reappearance of former living personages. They affect life and evolution. When did the first moment come? The first rate of vibration determines the subsequent ones. When man leaves the globe the forces die. Convulsions and cataclysms. Reincarnation and karma intermixed with cyclic law. Civilizations cycle back. The cycle of Avatars. Krishna, Buddha, and others come under cycles. Minor personages and great leaders. Intersection of cycles causes convulsions. The Moon, Sun, and Sidereal cycles. Individual cycles and that of reincarnation. The motion through the constellations, and the meaning of the story of Jonah. The Zodiacal clock. How the ideas are impressed and preserved by nations. Cause for earthquakes, Cosmic Fire, Glaciation, and Floods. The Brahmanical Cycles. Pages 132 to 143.

CHAPTER XV

DIFFERENTIATION OF SPECIES — MISSING LINKS

Ultimate origin of man not discoverable. Man not derived from a single pair, nor from the animals. Seven races of men appeared simultaneously on the globe. They are now amalgamated and will differentiate. The Anthropoid Apes. Their origin. They came from man. They are the descendants of offspring from unnatural union in the third and fourth races. The Delayed Races. The secret books on the question. Human features of apes accounted for. The lower kingdoms from other planets. Their differentiation by intelligent interference by the Dhyanis. The midway point of evolution. Astral forms of old rounds solidified in physical rounds. Missing links, what they are and why Science cannot discover them. The aim of Nature in all this work.
Pages 144 to 151.

CHAPTER XVI

PSYCHIC LAWS, FORCES, AND PHENOMENA

No true psychology in the West. It exists in the Orient. Man the mirror of all forces. Gravitation only a half law. Importance of polarity and cohesion. Rendering objects invisible. Imagination all powerful. Mental telegraphy. Reading minds is burglary. Apportation, clairvoyance, clairaudience, and second-sight. Pictures in the Astral Light. Dreams and visions. Apparitions. Real clairvoyance. Inner stimulus makes outer impression. Astral Light the Register of everything. Pages 152 to 164.

CHAPTER XVII

PSYCHIC PHENOMENA AND SPIRITUALISM

Spiritualism wrongly named. Should be called necromancy and the worship of the dead. This cult did not originate in America. The practice long known in India. The facts recorded deserve examination. Theosophists admit the facts but interpret them differently from the "spiritualist." The examination confined to the question of whether the dead return. The dead do not return thus. The mass of communications are from the astral shell of man. Objections stated to the claims made by mediums. The record justifies the ridicule of science. Materialization and what it is. A mass of electric magnetic matter with a picture upon it from the astral light. Or it is the astral body of the medium extruded from the living body. Analysis of the laws to be known before the phenomena can be understood. The *timbre* of the "independent voice." Importance of the astral realm. The Dangers of mediumship. Attempt to get these powers for money or selfish ends also dangerous. Cyclic law ordains the slackening of the force at this time. The purpose of the Lodge. Pages 165 to 173.

CHAPTER I
Theosophy and the Masters

THEOSOPHY is that ocean of knowledge which spreads from shore to shore of the evolution of sentient beings; unfathomable in its deepest parts, it gives the greatest minds their fullest scope, yet, shallow enough at its shores, it will not overwhelm the understanding of a child. It is wisdom about God for those who believe that he is all things and in all, and wisdom about nature for the man who accepts the statement found in the Christian Bible that God cannot be measured or discovered, and that darkness is around his pavilion. Although it contains by derivation the name God and thus may seem at first sight to embrace religion alone, it does not neglect science, for it is the science of sciences and therefore has been called the wisdom religion. For no science is complete which leaves out any department of nature, whether visible or invisible, and that religion which, depending solely on an assumed revelation, turns away from things and the laws which govern them is nothing but a delusion, a foe to progress, an obstacle in the way of man's advancement toward happiness. Embracing both the scientific and the religious, Theosophy is a scientific religion and a religious science.

It is not a belief or dogma formulated or invented by man, but is a knowledge of the laws which govern the evolution of the physical, astral, psychical, and intellectual constituents of nature and of man. The religion of the day is but a series of dogmas man-made and with no scientific foundation for promulgated ethics; while our science as yet ignores the unseen, and failing to admit the existence of a complete set of inner faculties of perception in man, it is cut off from the immense and real field of experience which lies within the visible and tangible worlds. But Theosophy knows that the whole is constituted of the visible and the invisible, and perceiving outer things and objects to be but transitory it grasps the facts of nature, both without and within. It is therefore complete in itself and sees no unsolvable mystery anywhere; it throws the word coincidence out of its vocabulary and hails the reign of law in everything and every circumstance.

That man possesses an immortal soul is the common belief of humanity; to this Theosophy adds that he is a soul; and further that all nature is sentient, that the vast array of objects and men are not mere collections of atoms fortuitously thrown together and thus without law evolving law, but down to the smallest atom all is soul and spirit ever evolving under the rule of law which is inherent in the whole. And just as the ancients taught, so does Theosophy; that the course of evolution is the drama of the soul and that nature exists for no other purpose than the soul's experience. The Theosophist agrees with Prof. Huxley in the assertion that there must be beings in the universe whose intelligence is as much beyond ours as ours exceeds that of the black beetle, and who take an active part in the government of the natural order of things. Pushing further on by the light of the confidence had in his teachers, the Theosophist adds that such intelligences were once human and came like all of us from other and previous worlds, where as varied experience had been gained as is possible on this one. We are therefore not appearing for the first time when we come upon this planet, but have pursued a long, an immeasurable course of activity and intelligent perception on other systems of globes, some of which were destroyed ages before the solar system condensed. This immense reach of the evolutionary system means, then, that this planet on which we now are is the result of the activity and the evolution of some other one that died long ago, leaving its energy to be used in the bringing into existence of the earth, and that the inhabitants of the latter in their turn came from some older world to proceed here with the destined work in matter. And the brighter planets, such as Venus, are the habitation of still more progressed entities, once as low as ourselves, but now raised up to a pitch of glory incomprehensible for our intellects.

The most intelligent being in the universe, man, has never, then, been without a friend, but has a line of elder brothers who continually watch over the progress of the less progressed, preserve the knowledge gained through æons of trial and experience, and continually seek for opportunities of drawing the developing intelligence of the race on this or other globes to consider the great truths concerning the destiny of the soul. These elder brothers also keep the knowledge they have gained of the laws of nature in all departments, and are ready when cyclic law permits to use it for the benefit of mankind. They have always existed as a body, all knowing each other, no matter in what part of the world they may be, and all working for the race in many different ways. In some periods they are well known to the people and move among ordinary men whenever the social organization, the virtue, and the development of the nations permit it. For if they were to come out openly and be heard of everywhere, they would be worshipped as gods by some and hunted as devils by others. In those periods when they do come out some of their number are rulers of men, some teachers, a few great philosophers, while others remain still unknown except to the most advanced of the body.

It would be subversive of the ends they have in view were they to make themselves public in the present civilization, which is based almost wholly on money, fame, glory, and personality. For this age, as one of them has already said, "is an age of transition," when every system of thought, science, religion, government, and society is changing, and men's minds are only preparing for an alteration into that state which will permit the race to advance to the point suitable for these elder brothers to introduce their actual presence to our sight. They may be truly called the bearers of the torch of truth across the ages; they investigate all things and beings; they know what man is in his innermost nature and what his powers and destiny, his state before birth and the states into which he goes after the death of his body; they have stood by the cradle of nations and seen the vast achievements of the ancients, watched sadly the decay of those who had no power to resist the cyclic law of rise and fall; and while cataclysms seemed to show a universal destruction of art, architecture, religion, and philosophy, they have preserved the records of it all in places secure from the ravages of either men or time; they have made minute observations, through trained psychics among their own order, into the unseen realms of nature and of mind, recorded the observations and preserved the record; they have mastered the mysteries of sound and color through which alone the elemental beings behind the veil of matter can be communicated with, and thus can tell why the rain falls and what it falls for, whether the earth is hollow or not, what makes the wind to blow and light to shine, and greater feat than all — one which implies a knowledge of the very foundations of nature — they know what the ultimate divisions of time are and what are the meaning and the times of the cycles.

But, asks the busy man of the nineteenth century who reads the newspapers and believes in "modern progress," if these elder brothers are all you claim them to be, why have they left no mark on history nor gathered men around them? Their own reply, published some time ago by Mr. A. P. Sinnett, is better than any I could write.

"We will first discuss, if you please, the one relating to the presumed failure of the 'Fraternity' to 'leave any mark upon the history of the world.' They ought, you think, to have been able, with their extraordinary advantages, to have 'gathered into their schools a considerable portion of the more enlightened minds of every race.' How do you know they have made no such mark? Are you acquainted with their efforts, successes, and failures? Have you any dock upon which to arraign them? How could your world collect proofs of the doings of men who have sedulously kept closed every possible door of approach by which the inquisitive could spy upon them? The prime condition of their success was that they should never be supervised or obstructed. What they have done they know; all that those outside their circle could perceive was results, the causes of which were masked from view. To account for these results, men have, in different ages, invented theories of the interposition of gods, special providences, fates, the benign or hostile influences of the stars. There never was a time within or before the so-called historical period when our predecessors were not moulding events and 'making history,' the facts of which were subsequently and invariably distorted by historians to suit contemporary prejudices. Are you quite sure that the visible heroic figures in the successive dramas were not often but their puppets? We never pretended to be able to draw nations in the mass to this or that crisis in spite of the general drift of the world's cosmic relations. The cycles must run their rounds. Periods of mental and moral light and darkness succeed each other as day does night. The major and minor yugas must be accomplished according to the established order of things. And we, borne along on the mighty tide, can only modify and direct some of its minor currents."

It is under cyclic law, during a dark period in the history of mind, that the true philosophy disappears for a time, but the same law causes it to reappear as surely as the sun rises and the human mind is present to see it. But some works can only be performed by the Master, while other works require the assistance of the companions. It is the Master's work to preserve the true philosophy, but the help of the companions is needed to rediscover and promulgate it. Once more the elder brothers have indicated where the truth — Theosophy — could be found, and the companions all over the world are engaged in bringing it forth for wider currency and propagation.

The Elder Brothers of Humanity are men who were perfected in former periods of evolution. These periods of manifestation are unknown to modern evolutionists so far as their number are concerned, though long ago understood by not only the older Hindus, but also by those great minds and men who instituted and carried on the first pure and undebased form of the Mysteries of Greece. The periods, when out of the Great Unknown there come forth the visible universes, are eternal in their coming and going, alternating with equal periods of silence and rest again in the Unknown. The object of these mighty waves is the production of perfect man, the evolution of soul, and they always witness the increase of the number of Elder Brothers; the life of the least of men pictures them in day and night, waking and sleeping, birth and death, "for these two, light and dark, day and night, are the world's eternal ways."

In every age and complete national history these men of power and compassion are given different designations. They have been called Initiates, Adepts, Magi, Hierophants, Kings of the East, Wise Men, Brothers, and what not. But in the Sanskrit language there is a word which, being applied to them, at once thoroughly identifies them with humanity. It is Mahatma. This is composed of *Maha* great, and *Atma* soul; so it means great soul, and as all men are souls the distinction of the Mahatma lies in greatness. The term Mahatma has come into wide use through the Theosophical Society, as Mme. H. P. Blavatsky constantly referred to them as her Masters who gave her the knowledge she possessed. They were at first known only as the Brothers, but afterwards, when many Hindus flocked to the Theosophical movement, the name Mahatma was brought into use, inasmuch as it has behind it an immense body of Indian tradition and literature. At different times unscrupulous enemies of the Theosophical Society have said that even this name had been invented and that such beings are not known of among the Indians or in their literature. But these assertions are made only to discredit if possible a philosophical movement that threatens to completely upset prevailing erroneous theological dogmas. For all through Hindu literature Mahatmas are often spoken of, and in parts of the north of that country the term is common. In the very old poem the *Bhagavad-Gītā,* revered by all Hindu sects and admitted by the western critics to be noble as well as beautiful, there is a verse reading, "Such a Mahatma is difficult to find."

But irrespective of all disputes as to specific names, there is sufficient argument and proof to show that a body of men having the wonderful knowledge described above has always existed and probably exists today. The older mysteries continually refer to them. Ancient Egypt had them in her great king-Initiates, sons of the sun and friends of great gods. There is a habit of belittling the ideas of the ancients which is in itself belittling to the people of today. Even the Christian who reverently speaks of Abraham as "the friend of God," will scornfully laugh at the idea of the claims of Egyptian rulers to the same friendship being other than childish assumption of dignity and title. But the truth is, these great Egyptians were Initiates, members of the one great lodge which includes all others of whatever degree or operation. The later and declining Egyptians, of course, must have imitated their predecessors, but that was when the true doctrine was beginning once more to be obscured upon the rise of dogma and priesthood.

The story of Apollonius of Tyana is about a member of one of the same ancient orders appearing among men at a descending cycle, and only for the purpose of keeping a witness upon the scene for future generations.

Abraham and Moses of the Jews are two other Initiates, Adepts who had their work to do with a certain people; and in the history of Abraham we meet with Melchizedek, who was so much beyond Abraham that he had the right to confer upon the latter a dignity, a privilege, or a blessing. The same chapter of human history which contains the names of Moses and Abraham is illuminated also by that of Solomon. And thus these three make a great Triad of Adepts, the record of whose deeds can not be brushed aside as folly and devoid of basis.

Moses was educated by the Egyptians and in Midian, from both of which he gained much occult knowledge, and any clear-seeing student of the great Universal Masonry can perceive all through his books the hand, the plan, and the work of a master. Abraham again knew all the arts and much of the power in psychical realms that were cultivated in his day, or else he could not have consorted with kings nor have been "the friend of God"; and the reference to his conversations with the Almighty in respect to the destruction of cities alone shows him to have been an Adept who had long ago passed beyond the need of ceremonial or other adventitious aids. Solomon completes this triad and stands out in characters of fire. Around him is clustered such a mass of legend and story about his dealings with the elemental powers and of his magic possessions that one must condemn the whole ancient world as a collection of fools who made lies for amusement if a denial is made of his being a great character, a wonderful example of the incarnation among men of a powerful Adept. We do not have to accept the name Solomon nor the pretense that he reigned over the Jews, but we must admit the fact that somewhere in the misty time to which the Jewish records refer there lived and moved among the people of the earth one who was an Adept and given that name afterwards. Peripatetics and microscopic critics may affect to see in the prevalence of universal tradition naught but evidence of the gullibility of men and their power to imitate, but the true student of human nature and life knows that the universal tradition is true and arises from the facts in the history of man.

Turning to India, so long forgotten and ignored by the lusty and egotistical, the fighting and the trading West, we find her full of the lore relating to these wonderful men of whom Noah, Abraham, Moses, and Solomon are only examples. There the people are fitted by temperament and climate to be the preservers of the philosophical, ethical, and psychical jewels that would have been forever lost to us had they been left to the ravages of such Goths and Vandals as western nations were in the early days of their struggle for education and civilization. If the men who wantonly burned up vast masses of historical and ethnological treasures found by the minions of the Catholic rulers of Spain, in Central and South America, could have known of and put their hands upon the books and palm-leaf records of India before the protecting shield of England was raised against them, they would have destroyed them all as they did for the Americans, and as their predecessors attempted to do for the Alexandrian library. Fortunately events worked otherwise.

All along the stream of Indian literature we can find the names by scores of great adepts who were well known to the people and who all taught the same story — the great epic of the human soul. Their names are unfamiliar to western ears, but the records of their thoughts, their work and powers remain. Still more, in the quiet unmoveable East there are today by the hundred persons who know of their own knowledge that the Great Lodge still exists and has its Mahatmas, Adepts, Initiates, Brothers. And yet further, in that land are such a number of experts in the practical application of minor though still very astonishing power over nature and her forces, that we have an irresistible mass of human evidence to prove the proposition laid down.

And if Theosophy — the teaching of this Great Lodge — is as said, both scientific and religious, then from the ethical side we have still more proof. A mighty Triad acting on and through ethics is that composed of Buddha, Confucius, and Jesus. The first, a Hindu, founds a religion which today embraces many more people than Christianity, teaching centuries before Jesus the ethics which he taught and which had been given out even centuries before Buddha. Jesus coming to reform his people repeats these ancient ethics, and Confucius does the same thing for ancient and honorable China.

The Theosophist says that all these great names represent members of the one single brotherhood, who all have a single doctrine. And the extraordinary characters who now and again appear in western civilization, such as St. Germain, Jacob Boehme, Cagliostro, Paracelsus, Mesmer, Count St. Martin, and Madame H. P. Blavatsky, are agents for the doing of the work of the Great Lodge at the proper time. It is true they are generally reviled and classed as impostors — though no one can find out why they are when they generally confer benefits and lay down propositions or make discoveries of great value to science after they have died. But Jesus himself would be called an impostor today if he appeared in some Fifth Avenue theatrical church rebuking the professed Christians. Paracelsus was the originator of valuable methods and treatments in medicine now universally used. Mesmer taught hypnotism under another name. Madame Blavatsky brought once more to the attention of the West the most important system, long known to the Lodge, respecting man, his nature and destiny. But all are alike called impostors by a people who have no original philosophy of their own and whose mendicant and criminal classes exceed in misery and in number those of any civilization on the earth.

It will not be unusual for nearly all occidental readers to wonder how men could possibly know so much and have such power over the operations of natural law as I have ascribed to the Initiates, now so commonly spoken of as the Mahatmas. In India, China, and other Oriental lands no wonder would arise on these heads, because there, although everything of a material civilization is just now in a backward state, they have never lost a belief in the inner nature of man and in the power he may exercise if he will. Consequently living examples of such powers and capacities have not been absent from those people. But in the West a materialistic civilization having arisen through a denial of the soul life and nature consequent upon a reaction from illogical dogmatism, there has not been any investigation of these subjects and, until lately, the general public has not believed in the possibility of anyone save a supposed God having such power.

A Mahatma endowed with power over space, time, mind, and matter, is a possibility just because he is a perfected man. Every human being has the germ of all the powers attributed to these great Initiates, the difference lying solely in the fact that we have in general not developed what we possess the germ of, while the Mahatma has gone through the training and experience which have caused all the unseen human powers to develop in him, and conferred gifts that look god-like to his struggling brother below. Telepathy, mind-reading, and hypnotism, all long ago known to Theosophy, show the existence in the human subject of planes of consciousness, functions, and faculties hitherto undreamed of. Mind-reading and the influencing of the mind of the hypnotized subject at a distance prove the existence of a mind which is not wholly dependent upon a brain, and that a medium exists through which the influencing thought may be sent. It is under this law that the Initiates can communicate with each other at no matter what distance. Its *rationale,* not yet admitted by the schools of the hypnotizers, is, that if the two minds vibrate or change into the same state they will think alike, or, in other words, the one who is to hear at a distance receives the impression sent by the other. In the same way with all other powers, no matter how extraordinary. They are all natural, although now unusual, just as great musical ability is natural though not usual or common. If an Initiate can make a solid object move without contact, it is because he understands the two laws of attraction and repulsion of which "gravitation" is but the name for one; if he is able to precipitate out of the viewless air the carbon which we know is in it, forming the carbon into sentences upon the paper, it is through his knowledge of the occult higher chemistry, and the use of a trained and powerful image making faculty which every man possesses; if he reads your thoughts with ease, that results from the use of the inner and only real powers of sight, which require no retina to see the fine-pictured web which the vibrating brain of man weaves about him. All that the Mahatma may do is natural to the perfected man; but if those powers are not at once revealed to us it is because the race is as yet selfish altogether and still living for the present and the transitory.

I repeat then, that though the true doctrine disappears for a time from among men it is bound to reappear, because first, it is impacted in the imperishable center of man's nature; and secondly, the Lodge forever preserves it, not only in actual objective records, but also in the intelligent and fully self-conscious men who, having successfully overpassed the many periods of evolution which preceded the one we are now involved in, cannot lose the precious possessions they have acquired. And because the elder brothers are the highest product of evolution through whom alone, in cooperation with the whole human family, the further regular and workmanlike prosecution of the plans of the Great Architect of the Universe could be carried on, I have thought it well to advert to them and their Universal Lodge before going to other parts of the subject.

CHAPTER II
General Principles

THE teachings of Theosophy deal for the present chiefly with our earth, although its purview extends to all the worlds, since no part of the manifested universe is outside the single body of laws which operate upon us. Our globe being one of the solar system is certainly connected with Venus, Jupiter, and other planets, but as the great human family has to remain with its material vehicle — the earth — until all the units of the race which are ready are perfected, the evolution of that family is of greater importance to the members of it. Some particulars respecting the other planets may be given later on. First let us take a general view of the laws governing all.

The universe evolves from the unknown, into which no man or mind, however high, can inquire, on seven planes or in seven ways or methods in all worlds, and this sevenfold differentiation causes all the worlds of the universe and the beings thereon to have a septenary constitution. As was taught of old, the little worlds and the great are copies of the whole, and the minutest insect as well as the most highly developed being are *replicas* in little or in great of the vast inclusive original. Hence sprang the saying, "as above so below" which the Hermetic philosophers used.

The divisions of the sevenfold universe may be laid down roughly as: The Absolute, Spirit, Mind, Matter, Will, Akasa or Æther, and Life. In place of "the Absolute" we can use the word Space. For Space is that which ever is, and in which all manifestation must take place. The term Akasa, taken from the Sanskrit, is used in place of Æther, because the English language has not yet evolved a word to properly designate that tenuous state of matter which is now sometimes called Ether by modern scientists. As to the Absolute we can do no more than say It Is. None of the great teachers of the School ascribe qualities to the Absolute although all the qualities exist in It. Our knowledge begins with differentiation, and all manifested objects, beings, or powers are only differentiations of the Great Unknown. The most that can be said is that the Absolute periodically differentiates itself, and periodically withdraws the differentiated into itself.

The first differentiation — speaking metaphysically as to time — is Spirit, with which appears Matter and Mind. Akasa is produced from Matter and Spirit, Will is the force of Spirit in action and Life is a resultant of the action of Akasa, moved by Spirit, upon Matter.

But the Matter here spoken of is not that which is vulgarly known as such. It is the real Matter which is always invisible, and has sometimes been called Primordial Matter. In the Brahmanical system it is denominated *Mulaprakriti.* The ancient teaching always held, as is now admitted by Science, that we see or perceive only the phenomena but not the essential nature, body or being of matter.

Mind is the intelligent part of the Cosmos, and in the collection of seven differentiations above roughly sketched, Mind is that in which the plan of the Cosmos is fixed or contained. This plan is brought over from a prior period of manifestation which added to its ever-increasing perfectness, and no limit can be set to its evolutionary possibilities in perfectness, because there was never any beginning to the periodical manifestations of the Absolute, there never will be any end, but forever the going forth and withdrawing into the Unknown will go on.

Wherever a world or system of worlds is evolving there the plan has been laid down in universal mind, the original force comes from spirit, the basis is matter — which is in fact invisible — Life sustains all the forms requiring life, and Akasa is the connecting link between matter on one side and spirit-mind on the other.

When a world or a system comes to the end of certain great cycles men record a cataclysm in history or tradition. These traditions abound; among the Jews in their flood; with the Babylonians in theirs; in Egyptian papyri; in the Hindu cosmology; and none of them as merely confirmatory of the little Jewish tradition, but all pointing to early teaching and dim recollection also of the periodical destructions and renovations. The Hebraic story is but a poor fragment torn from the pavement of the Temple of Truth. Just as there are periodical minor cataclysms or partial destructions, so, the doctrine holds, there is the universal evolution and involution. Forever the Great Breath goes forth and returns again. As it proceeds outwards, objects, worlds and men appear; as it recedes all disappear into the original source.

This is the waking and the sleeping of the Great Being; the Day and the Night of Brahma; the prototype of our waking days and sleeping nights as men, of our disappearance from the scene at the end of one little human life, and our return again to take up the unfinished work in another life, in a new day.

The real age of the world has long been involved in doubt for Western investigators, who up to the present have shown a singular unwillingness to take instruction from the records of Oriental people much older than the West. Yet with the Orientals is the truth about the matter. It is admitted that Egyptian civilization flourished many centuries ago, and as there are no living Egyptian schools of ancient learning to offend modern pride, and perhaps because the Jews "came out of Egypt" to fasten the Mosaic misunderstood tradition upon modern progress, the inscriptions cut in rocks and written on papyri obtain a little more credit today than the living thought and record of the Hindus. For the latter are still among us, and it would never do to admit that a poor and conquered race possesses knowledge respecting the age of man and his world which the western flower of culture, war, and annexation knows nothing of. Ever since the ignorant monks and theologians of Asia Minor and Europe succeeded in imposing the Mosaic account of the genesis of earth and man upon the coming western evolution, the most learned even of our scientific men have stood in fear of the years that elapsed since Adam, or have been warped in thought and perception whenever their eyes turned to any chronology different from that of a few tribes of the sons of Jacob. Even the noble, aged, and silent pyramid of Gizeh, guarded by Sphinx and Memnon made of stone, has been degraded by Piazzi Smyth and others into a proof that the British inch must prevail and that a "Continental Sunday" controverts the law of the Most High. Yet in the Mosaic account, where one would expect to find a reference to such a proof as the pyramid, we can discover not a single hint of it and only a record of the building by King Solomon of a temple of which there never was a trace.

But the Theosophist knows why the Hebraic tradition came to be thus an apparent drag on the mind of the West; he knows the connection between Jew and Egyptian; what is and is to be the resurrection of the old pyramid builders of the Nile valley, and where the plans of those ancient master masons have been hidden from the profane eyes until the cycle should roll round again for their bringing forth. The Jews preserved merely a part of the learning of Egypt hidden under the letter of the books of Moses, and it is there still to this day in what they call the cabalistic or hidden meaning of the scriptures. But the Egyptian souls who helped in planning the pyramid of Gizeh, who took part in the Egyptian government, theology, science, and civilization, departed from their old race, that race died out and the former Egyptians took up their work in the oncoming races of the West, especially in those which are now repeopling the American continents. When Egypt and India were younger there was a constant intercourse between them. They both, in the opinion of the Theosophist, thought alike, but fate ruled that of the two the Hindus only should preserve the old ideas among a living people. I will therefore take from the Brahmanical records of Hindustan their doctrine about the days, nights, years and life of Brahma, who represents the universe and the worlds.

The doctrine at once upsets the interpretation so long given to the Mosaic tradition, but fully accords with the evident account in Genesis of other and former "creations," with the cabalistic construction of the Old Testament verse about the kings of Edom, who there represent former periods of evolution prior to that started with Adam, and also coincides with the belief held by some of the early Christian Fathers who told their brethren about wonderful previous worlds and creations.

The Day of Brahma is said to last one thousand years, and his night is of equal length. In the Christian Bible is a verse saying that one day is as a thousand years to the Lord and a thousand years as one day. This has generally been used to magnify the power of Jehovah, but it has a suspicious resemblance to the older doctrine of the length of Brahma's day and night. It would be of more value if construed to be a statement of the periodical coming forth for great days and nights of equal length of the universe of manifested worlds.

A day of mortals is reckoned by the sun, and is but twelve hours in length. On Mercury it would be different, and on Saturn or Uranus still more so. But a day of Brahma is made up of what are called Manvantaras — or period between two men — fourteen in number. These include four billion three hundred and twenty million mortal, or earth, years, which is one day of Brahma.

When this day opens, cosmic evolution, so far as relates to this solar system, begins and occupies between one and two billions of years in evolving the very ethereal first matter before the astral kingdoms of mineral, vegetable, animal and men are possible. This second step takes some three hundred millions of years, and then still more material processes go forward for the production of the tangible kingdoms of nature, including man. This covers over one and one-half billions of years. And the number of solar years included in the present "human" period is over eighteen millions of years.

This is exactly what Herbert Spencer designates as the gradual coming forth of the known and heterogeneous from the unknown and homogeneous. For the ancient Egyptian and Hindu Theosophists never admitted a creation out of nothing, but ever strenuously insisted upon evolution, by gradual stages, of the heterogeneous and differentiated from the homogeneous and undifferentiated. No mind can comprehend the infinite and absolute unknown, which is, has no beginning and shall have no end; which is both last and first, because, whether differentiated or withdrawn into itself, it ever is. This is the God spoken of in the Christian Bible as the one around whose pavilion there is darkness.

This cosmic and human chronology of the Hindus is laughed at by western Orientalists, yet they can furnish nothing better and are continually disagreeing with each other on the same subject. In Wilson's translation of *Vishnu Purana* he calls it all fiction based on nothing, and childish boasting. But the Free Masons, who remain inactive hereupon, ought to know better. They could find in the story of the building of Solomon's temple from the heterogeneous materials brought from everywhere, and its erection without the noise of a tool being heard, the agreement with these ideas of their Egyptian and Hindu brothers. For Solomon's Temple means man whose frame is built up, finished and decorated without the least noise. But the materials had to be found, gathered together and fashioned in other and distant places. These are in the periods above spoken of, very distant and very silent. Man could not have his bodily temple to live in until all the matter in and about his world had been found by the Master, who is the inner man; when found the plans for working it required to be detailed. They then had to be carried out in different detail until all the parts should be perfectly ready and fit for placing in the final structure. So in the vast stretch of time which began after the first almost intangible matter had been gathered and kneaded, the material and vegetable kingdoms had sole possession here with the Master — man — who was hidden from sight within carrying forward the plans for the foundations of the human temple. All of this requires many, many ages, since we know that nature never leaps. And when the rough work was completed, when the human temple was erected, many more ages would be required for all the servants, the priests, and the counsellors to learn their parts properly so that man, the Master, might be able to use the temple for its best and highest purposes.

The ancient doctrine is far nobler than the Christian religious one or that of the purely scientific school. The religious gives a theory which conflicts with reason and fact, while science can give for the facts which it observes no reason which is in any way noble or elevating. Theosophy alone, inclusive of all systems and every experience, gives the key, the plan, the doctrine, the truth.

The real age of the world is asserted by Theosophy to be almost incalculable, and that of man as he is now formed is over eighteen millions of years. What has become at last man is of vastly greater age, for before the present two sexes appeared the human creature was sometimes of one shape and sometimes of another, until the whole plan had been fully worked out into our present form, function, and capacity. This is found to be referred to in the ancient books written for the profane where man is said to have been at one time globular in shape. This was at a time when the conditions favored such a form and of course it was longer ago than eighteen millions of years. And when this globular form was the rule the sexes as we know them had not differentiated and hence there was but one sex, or if you like, no sex at all.

During all these ages before our man came into being, evolution was carrying on the work of perfecting various powers which are now our possession. This was accomplished by the Ego or real man going through experience in countless conditions of matter all different one from the other, and the same plan in general was and is pursued as prevails in respect to the general evolution of the universe to which I have before adverted. That is, details were first worked out in spheres of being very ethereal, metaphysical in fact. Then the next step brought the same details to be worked out on a plane of matter a little more dense, until at last it could be done on our present plane of what we miscall gross matter. In these anterior states the senses existed in germ, as it were, or in idea, until the astral plane which is next to this one was arrived at, and then they were concentrated so as to be the actual senses we now use through the agency of the different outer organs. These outer organs of sight, touch and hearing, and tasting, are often mistaken by the unlearned or the thoughtless for the real organs and senses, but he who stops to think must see that the senses are interior and that their outer organs are

real senses are within (soul)

but mediators between the visible universe and the real perceiver within. And all these various powers and potentialities being well worked out in this slow but sure process, at last man is put upon the scene a sevenfold being just as the universe and earth itself are sevenfold. Each of his seven principles is derived from one of the great first seven divisions, and each relates to a planet or scene of evolution, and to a race in which that evolution was carried out. So the first sevenfold differentiation is important to be borne in mind, since it is the basis of all that follows; just as the universal evolution is septenary so the evolution of humanity, sevenfold in its constitution, is carried on upon a septenary Earth. This is spoken of in Theosophical literature as the Sevenfold Planetary Chain, and is intimately connected with Man's special evolution.

CHAPTER II

CHAPTER III
The Earth Chain

COMING now to our Earth the view put forward by Theosophy regarding its genesis, its evolution and the evolution of the Human, Animal and other Monads, is quite different from modern ideas, and in some things contrary to accepted theories. But the theories of today are not stable. They change with each century, while the Theosophical one never alters because, in the opinion of those Elder Brothers who have caused its repromulgation and pointed to its confirmation in ancient books, it is but a statement of facts in nature. The modern theory is, on the contrary, always speculative, changeable, and continually altered.

Following the general plan outlined in preceding pages, the Earth is sevenfold. It is an entity and not a mere lump of gross matter. And being thus an entity of a septenary nature there must be six other globes which roll with it in space. This company of seven globes has been called the "Earth Chain," the "Planetary Chain." In *Esoteric Buddhism* this is clearly stated, but there a rather hard and fast materialistic view of it is given and the reader led to believe that the doctrine speaks of seven distinct globes, all separated from though connected with each other. One is forced to conclude that the author meant to say that the globe Earth is as distinct from the other six as Venus is from Mars.

This is not the doctrine. The earth is one of seven

globes, in respect to man's consciousness only, because when he functions on one of the seven he perceives it as a distinct globe and does not see the other six. This is in perfect correspondence with man himself who has six other constituents of which only the gross body is visible to him because he is now functioning on the Earth — or the fourth globe — and his body represents the Earth. The whole seven "globes" constitute one single mass or great globe and they all interpenetrate each other. But we have to say "globe," because the ultimate shape is globular or spherical. If one relies too closely on the explanation made by Mr. Sinnett it might be supposed that the globes did not interpenetrate each other but were connected by currents or lines of magnetic force. And if too close attention is paid to the diagrams used in the *Secret Doctrine* to illustrate the scheme, without paying due regard to the explanations and cautions given by H. P. Blavatsky, the same error may be made. But both she and her Adept teachers say, that the seven globes of our chain are in *"coadunation with each other but not in consubstantiality."** This is further enforced by cautions not to rely on statistics or plane surface diagrams, but to look at the metaphysical and spiritual aspect of the theory as stated in English. Thus from the very source of Mr. Sinnett's book we have the statement, that these globes are united in one mass though differing from each other in substance, and that this difference of substance is due to change of center of consciousness.

The Earth Chain of seven globes as thus defined is the direct reincarnation of a former chain of seven globes, and

* *Secret Doctrine,* Vol. I, p. 166, first edition.

that former family of seven was the moon chain, the moon itself being the visible representative of the fourth globe of the old chain. When that former vast entity composed of the Moon and six others, all united in one mass, reached its limit of life it died just as any being dies. Each one of the seven sent its energies into space and gave similar life or vibration to cosmic dust — matter, — and the total cohesive force of the whole kept the seven energies together. This resulted in the evolving of the present Earth Chain of seven centers of energy or evolution combined in one mass. As the Moon was the fourth of the old series it is on the same plane of perception as the Earth, and as we are now confined in our consciousness largely to Earth we are able only to see one of the old seven — to wit: our Moon. When we are functioning on any of the other seven we will perceive in our sky the corresponding old corpse which will then be a Moon, and we will not see the present Moon. Venus, Mars, Mercury and other visible planets are all fourth-plane globes of distinct planetary masses and for that reason are visible to us, their companion six centers of energy and consciousness being invisible. All diagrams on plane surfaces will only becloud the theory because a diagram necessitates linear divisions.

The stream or mass of Egos which evolves on the seven globes of our chain is limited in number, yet the actual quantity is enormous. For though the universe is limitless and infinite, yet in any particular portion of Cosmos in which manifestation and evolution have begun there is a limit to the extent of manifestation and to the number of Egos engaged therein. And the whole number of Monads now going through evolution on our Earth Chain came over from the old seven planets or globes which I have described. *Esoteric Buddhism* calls this mass of Egos a "life wave," meaning the stream of Monads. It reached this planetary mass, represented to our consciousness by the central point our Earth, and began on Globe A or No. 1, coming like an army or river. The first portion began on Globe A and went through a long evolution there in bodies suited to such a state of matter, and then passed on to B, and so on through the whole seven greater states of consciousness which have been called globes. When the first portion left A others streamed in and pursued the same course, the whole army proceeding with regularity round the septenary route.

This journey went on for four circlings round the whole, and then the whole stream or army of Egos from the old Moon Chain had arrived, and being complete, no more entered after the middle of the Fourth Round. The same circling process of these differently arrived classes goes on for seven complete Rounds of the whole seven planetary centers of consciousness, and when the seven are ended as much perfection as is possible in the immense period occupied will have been attained, and then this chain or mass of "globes" will die in its turn to give birth to still another series.

Each one of the globes is used by evolutionary law for the development of seven races, and of senses, faculties and powers appropriate to that state of matter: the experience of the whole seven globes being needed to make a perfect development. Hence we have the Rounds and Races. The Round is a circling of the seven centers of planetary consciousness; the Race the racial development on one of those seven. There are seven races for each globe, but the total of forty-nine races only makes up seven great races, the special septennate of races on each globe or planetary center composing in reality one race of seven constituents or special peculiarities of function and power.

And as no complete race could be evolved in a moment on any globe, the slow, orderly processes of nature, which allow no jumps, must proceed by appropriate means. Hence sub-races have to be evolved one after the other before the perfect root race is formed, and then the root race sends off its offshoots while it is declining and preparing for the advent of the next great race.

As illustrating this, it is distinctly taught that on the Americas is to be evolved the new — sixth — race; and here all the races of the earth are now engaged in a great amalgamation from which will result a very highly developed sub-race, after which others will be evolved by similar processes until the new one is completed.

Between the end of any great race and the beginning of another there is a period of rest, so far as the globe is concerned, for then the stream of human Egos leaves it for another one of the chain in order to go on with further evolution of powers and faculties there. But when the last, the seventh, race has appeared and fully perfected itself, a great dissolution comes on, similar to that which I briefly described as preceding the birth of the earth's chain, and then the world disappears as a tangible thing, and so far as the human ear is concerned there is silence. This, it is said, is the root of the belief so general that the world will come to an end, that there will be a judgment-day, or that there have been universal floods or fires.

Taking up evolution on the Earth, it is stated that the stream of Monads begins first to work up the mass of matter in what are called elemental conditions when all is gaseous or fiery. For the ancient and true theory is that no evolution is possible without the Monad as vivifying agent. In this first stage there is no animal or vegetable. Next comes the mineral when the whole mass hardens, the Monads being all imprisoned within. Then the first Monads emerge into vegetable forms which they construct themselves, and no animals yet appear. Next the first class of Monads emerges from the vegetable and produces the animal, then the human astral and shadowy model, and we have minerals, vegetables, animals and future men, for the second and later classes are still evolving in the lower kingdoms. When the middle of the Fourth Round is reached no more Monads emerge into the human stage and will not until a new planetary mass, reincarnated from ours, is made. This is the whole process roughly given, but with many details left out, for in one of the rounds man appears before the animals. But this detail need lead to no confusion.

And to state it in another way. The plan comes first in the universal mind, after which the astral model or basis is made, and when that astral model is completed, the whole process is gone over so as to condense the matter, up to the middle of the Fourth Round. Subsequent to that, which is our future, the whole mass is spiritualized with full consciousness and the entire body of globes raised up to a higher plane of development. In the process of condensing above referred to there is an alteration in respect to the time of the appearance of man on the planet. But as to these details the teachers have only said, "that at the Second Round the plan varies, but the variation will not be given to this generation." Hence it is impossible for me to give it. But there is no vagueness on the point that seven great races have to evolve here on this planet, and that the entire collection of races has to go seven times round the whole series of seven globes.

Human beings did not appear here in two sexes first. The first were of no sex, then they altered into hermaphrodite, and lastly separated into male and female. And this separation into male and female for human beings was over 18,000,000 years ago. For that reason is it said, in these ancient schools, that our humanity is 18,000,000 years old and a little over.

CHAPTER III

CHAPTER IV
Septenary Constitution of Man

RESPECTING the nature of man there are two ideas current in the religious circles of Christendom. One is the teaching and the other the common acceptation of it; the first is not secret, to be sure, in the Church, but it is so seldom dwelt upon in the hearing of the laity as to be almost arcane for the ordinary person. Nearly everyone says he has a soul and a body, and there it ends. What the soul is, and whether it is the real person or whether it has any powers of its own, are not inquired into, the preachers usually confining themselves to its salvation or damnation. And by thus talking of it as something different from oneself, the people have acquired an underlying notion that they are not souls because the soul may be lost by them. From this has come about a tendency to materialism causing men to pay more attention to the body than to the soul, the latter being left to the tender mercies of the priest of the Roman Catholics, and among dissenters the care of it is most frequently put off to the dying day. But when the true teaching is known it will be seen that the care of the soul, which is the Self, is a vital matter requiring attention every day, and not to be deferred without grievous injury resulting to the whole man, both soul and body.

The Christian teaching, supported by St. Paul, since upon him, in fact, dogmatic Christianity rests, is that man is composed of body, soul, and spirit. This is the threefold constitution of man, believed by the theologians but kept in the background because its examination might result in the readoption of views once orthodox but now heretical. For when we thus place soul between spirit and body, we come very close to the necessity for looking into the question of the soul's responsibility — since mere body can have no responsibility. And in order to make the soul responsible for the acts performed, we must assume that it has powers and functions. From this it is easy to take the position that the soul may be rational or irrational, as the Greeks sometimes thought, and then there is but a step to further Theosophical propositions. This threefold scheme of the nature of man contains, in fact, the Theosophical teaching of his sevenfold constitution, because the four other divisions missing from the category can be found in the powers and functions of body and soul, as I shall attempt to show later on. This conviction that man is a septenary and not merely a duad, was held long ago and very plainly taught to every one with accompanying demonstrations, but like other philosophical tenets it disappeared from sight, because gradually withdrawn at the time when in the east of Europe morals were degenerating and before materialism had gained full sway in company with scepticism, its twin. Upon its withdrawal the present dogma of body, soul, spirit, was left to Christendom. The reason for that concealment and its rejuvenescence in this century is well put by Mme. H. P. Blavatsky in the *Secret Doctrine.* In answer to the statement, "we cannot understand how any danger could arise from the revelation of such a purely philosophical doctrine as the evolution of the planetary chain," she says:

> The danger was this: Doctrines such as the Planetary chain or the seven races at once give a clue to the seven-fold nature of

man, for each principle is correlated to a plane, a planet, and a race; and the human principles are, on every plane, correlated to seven-fold occult forces — those of the higher planes being of tremendous occult powers, the abuse of which would cause incalculable evil to humanity. A clue, which is, perhaps, no clue to the present generation — especially the Westerns — protected as they are by their very blindness and ignorant materialistic disbelief in the occult; but a clue which would, nevertheless, have been very real in the early centuries of the Christian era, to people fully convinced of the reality of occultism, and entering a cycle of degradation, which made them rife [ripe] for abuse of occult powers and sorcery of the worst description.

Mr. A. P. Sinnett, at one time an official in the Government of India, first outlined in this century the real nature of man in his book *Esoteric Buddhism,* which was made up from information conveyed to him by H. P. Blavatsky directly from the Great Lodge of Initiates to which reference has been made. And in thus placing the old doctrine before western civilization he conferred a great benefit on his generation and helped considerably the cause of Theosophy. His classification was:

(1.) The Body, or *Rupa.*
(2.) Vitality, or *Prana-Jiva.*
(3.) Astral Body, or *Linga-Sarira.*
(4.) Animal Soul, or *Kama-Rupa.*
(5.) Human Soul, or *Manas.*
(6.) Spiritual Soul, or *Buddhi.*
(7.) Spirit, or *Atma.*

The words in italics being equivalents in the Sanskrit language adopted by him for the English terms. This classification stands to this day for all practical purposes, but it is capable of modification and extension. For instance, a later arrangement which places Astral body second instead of third in the category does not substantially alter it. It at once gives an idea of what man is, very different from the vague description by the words "body and soul," and also boldly challenges the materialistic conception that mind is the product of brain, a portion of the body. No claim is made that these principles were hitherto unknown, for they were all understood in various ways not only by the Hindus but by many Europeans. Yet the compact presentation of the sevenfold constitution of man in intimate connection with the septenary constitution of a chain of globes through which the being evolves, had not been given out. The French Abbé, Eliphas Levi, wrote about the astral realm and the astral body, but evidently had no knowledge of the remainder of the doctrine, and while the Hindus possessed the other terms in their language and philosophy, they did not use a septenary classification, but depended chiefly on a fourfold one and certainly concealed (if they knew of it) the doctrine of a chain of seven globes including our earth. Indeed, a learned Hindu, Subba Row, now deceased, asserted that they knew of a seven-fold classification, but that it had not been and would not be given out.

Considering these constituents in another manner, we would say that the lower man is a composite being, but in his real nature is a unity, or immortal being, comprising a trinity of Spirit, Discernment, and Mind which requires four lower mortal instruments or vehicles through which to work in matter and obtain experience from Nature. This trinity is that called *Atma-Buddhi-Manas* in Sanskrit, difficult terms to render in English. *Atma* is Spirit, *Buddhi* is the highest power of intellection, that which discerns and judges, and *Manas* is Mind. This threefold collection is the real man; and beyond doubt the doctrine is the origin of the theological one of the trinity of Father, Son, and Holy Ghost. The four lower instruments or vehicles are shown in this table:

Atma,	The Passions and Desires,
Buddhi,	Life Principle,
Manas,	Astral Body,
	Physical Body.

These four lower material constituents are transitory and subject to disintegration in themselves as well as to separation from each other. When the hour arrives for their separation to begin, the combination can no longer be kept up, the physical body dies, the atoms of which each of the four is composed begin to separate from each other, and the whole collection being disjointed is no longer fit for one as an instrument for the real man. This is what is called "death" among us mortals, but it is not death for the real man because he is deathless, persistent, immortal. He is therefore called the Triad, or indestructible trinity, while they are known as the Quaternary or mortal four.

This quaternary or lower man is a product of cosmic or physical laws and substance. It has been evolved during a lapse of ages, like any other physical thing, from cosmic substance, and is therefore subject to physical, physiological, and psychical laws which govern the race of man as a whole. Hence its period of possible continuance can be calculated just as the limit of tensile strain among the metals used in bridge building can be deduced by the engineer. Any one collection in the form of man made up of these constituents is therefore limited in duration by the laws of the evolutionary period in which it exists. Just now, that is generally seventy to one hundred years, but its possible duration is longer. Thus there are in history instances where ordinary persons have lived to be two hundred years of age; and by a knowledge of the occult laws of nature the possible limit of duration may be extended nearly to four hundred years.

The visible physical man is:
- Brain,
- Nerves,
- Blood,
- Bones,
- Lymph,
- Muscles,
- Organs of Sensation and Action,
- and Skin.

The unseen physical man is:
- Astral Body,
- Passions and Desires,
- Life Principle, (called *prana* or *jiva*).

It will be seen that the physical part of our nature is thus extended to a second department which, though invisible to the physical eye, is nevertheless material and subject to decay. Because people in general have been in the habit of admitting to be real only what they can see with the physical eye, they have at last come to suppose that the unseen is neither real nor material. But they forgot that even on the earth plane noxious gases are invisible though real and powerfully material, and that water may exist in the air held suspended and invisible until conditions alter and cause its precipitation.

Let us recapitulate before going into details. The *Real Man* is the trinity of *Atma-Buddhi-Manas,* or Spirit and Mind, and he uses certain agents and instruments to get in touch with nature in order to know himself. These instruments and agents are found in the lower Four — or the Quaternary — each principle in which category is of itself an instrument for the particular experience belonging to its own field, the body being the lowest, least important, and most transitory of the whole series. For when we arrive at the body on the way down from the Higher Mind, it can be shown that all of its organs are in themselves senseless and useless when deprived of the man within. Sight, hearing, touch, taste, and smelling do not pertain to the body but to the second unseen physical man, the real organs for the exercise of those powers being in the Astral Body, and those in the physical body being but the mechanical outer instruments for making the coordination between nature and the real organs inside.

CHAPTER V
Body and Astral Body

THE body, as a mass of flesh, bones, muscles, nerves, brain matter, bile, mucous, blood, and skin is an object of exclusive care for too many people, who make it their god because they have come to identify themselves with it, meaning it only when they say "I." Left to itself it is devoid of sense, and acts in such a case solely by reflex and automatic action. This we see in sleep, for then the body assumes attitudes and makes motions which the waking man does not permit. It is like mother earth in that it is made up of a number of infinitesimal "lives." Each of these lives is a sensitive point. Not only are there microbes, bacilli, and bacteria, but these are composed of others, and those others of still more minute lives. These lives are not the cells of the body, but make up the cells, keeping ever within the limits assigned by evolution to the cell. They are forever whirling and moving together throughout the whole body, being in certain apparently void spaces as well as where flesh, membrane, bones, and blood are seen. They extend, too, beyond the actual outer limits of the body to a measurable distance.

One of the mysteries of physical life is hidden among these "lives." Their action, forced forward by the Life energy — called *Prana* or *Jiva* — will explain active existence and physical death. They are divided into two classes, one the destroyers, the other the preservers, and these two war upon each other from birth until the destroyers win. In this struggle the Life Energy itself ends

see Index V

the contest because it is life that kills. This may seem heterodox, but in Theosophical philosophy it is held to be the fact. For, it is said, the infant lives because the combination of healthy organs is able to absorb the life all around it in space, and is put to sleep each day by the overpowering strength of the stream of life, since the preservers among the cells of the youthful body are not yet mastered by the other class. These processes of going to sleep and waking again are simply and solely the restoring of the equilibrium in sleep and the action produced by disturbing it when awake. It may be compared with the arc-electric light wherein the brilliant arc of light at the point of resistance is the symbol of the waking active man. So in sleep we are again absorbing and not resisting the Life Energy; when we wake we are throwing it off. But as it exists around us like an ocean in which we swim, our power to throw it off is necessarily limited. Just when we wake we are in equilibrium as to our organs and life; when we fall asleep we are yet more full of life than in the morning; it has exhausted us; it finally kills the body. Such a contest could not be waged forever, since the whole solar system's weight of life is pitted against the power to resist focussed in one small human frame.

The body is considered by the Masters of Wisdom to be the most transitory, impermanent, and illusionary of the whole series of constituents in man. Not for a moment is it the same. Ever changing, in motion in every part, it is in fact never complete or finished though tangible. The ancients clearly perceived this, for they elaborated a doctrine called Naimittika* Pralaya, or the continual change in

*[The correct Sanskrit term is *Nitya*.]

material things, the continual destruction. This is known now to science in the doctrine that the body undergoes a complete alteration and renovation every seven years. At the end of the first seven years it is not the same body it was in the beginning. At the end of our days it has changed seven times, perhaps more. And yet it presents the same general appearance from maturity until death; and it is a human form from birth to maturity. This is a mystery science explains not; it is a question pertaining to the cell and to the means whereby the general human shape is preserved.

The "cell" is an illusion. It is merely a word. It has no existence as a material thing, for any cell is composed of other cells. What, then, is a cell? It is the ideal form within which the actual physical atoms — made up of the "lives" — arrange themselves. As it is admitted that the physical molecules are forever rushing away from the body, they must be leaving the cells each moment. Hence there is no physical cell, but the privative limits of one, the ideal walls and general shape. The molecules assume position within the ideal shape according to the laws of nature, and leave it again almost at once to give place to other atoms. And as it is thus with the body, so is it with the earth and with the solar system. Thus also is it, though in slower measure, with all material objects. They are all in constant motion and change. This is modern and also ancient wisdom. This is the physical explanation of clairvoyance, clairaudience, telepathy, and mind-reading. It helps to show us what a deluding and unsatisfactory thing our body is.

Although, strictly speaking, the second constituent of

man is the Astral Body — called in Sanskrit *Linga Sarira* — we will consider Life Energy — or *Prana* and *Jiva* in Sanskrit — together, because to our observation the phenomenon of life is more plainly exhibited in connection with the body.

Life is not the result of the operation of the organs, nor is it gone when the body dissolves. It is a universally pervasive principle. It is the ocean in which the earth floats; it permeates the globe and every being and object on it. It works unceasingly on and around us, pulsating against and through us forever. When we occupy a body we merely use a more specialized instrument than any other for dealing with both *Prana* and *Jiva*. Strictly speaking, *Prana* is breath; and as breath is necessary for continuance of life in the human machine, that is the better word. *Jiva* means "life," and also is applied to the living soul, for the life in general is derived from the Supreme Life itself. *Jiva* is therefore capable of general application, whereas *Prana* is more particular. It cannot be said that one has a definite amount of this Life Energy which will fly back to its source should the body be burned, but rather that it works with whatever be the mass of matter in it. We, as it were, secrete or use it as we live. For whether we are alive or dead, life-energy is still there; in life among our organs sustaining them, in death among the innumerable creatures that arise from our destruction. We can no more do away with this life than we can erase the air in which the bird floats, and like the air it fills all the spaces on the planet, so that nowhere can we lose the benefit of it nor escape its final crushing power. But in working upon the physical body this life — *Prana*

The body is an instrument to use the life energy that is all around us and everything else

— needs a vehicle, means, or guide, and this vehicle is the astral body.

There are many names for the Astral Body. Here are a few: *Linga Sarira,* Sanskrit, meaning design body, and the best one of all; ethereal double; phantom; wraith; apparition; doppelgänger; personal man; perisprit; irrational soul; animal soul; *Bhuta*; elementary; spook; devil; demon. Some of these apply only to the astral body when devoid of the corpus after death. *Bhuta,* devil, and elementary are nearly synonymous; the first Sanskrit, the other English. With the Hindus the *Bhuta* is the Astral Body when it is by death released from the body and the mind; and being thus separated from conscience, is a devil in their estimation. They are not far wrong, if we abolish the old notion that a devil is an angel fallen from heaven, for this bodily devil is something which rises from the earth.

It may be objected that the term Astral Body is not the right one for this purpose. The objection is one which arises from the nature and genesis of the English language, for as that has grown up in a struggle with nature and among a commercial people it has not as yet coined the words needed for designating the great range of faculties and organs of the unseen man. And as its philosophers have not admitted the existence of these inner organs, the right terms do not exist in the language. So in looking for words to describe the inner body the only ones found in English were the "astral body." This term comes near to the real fact, since the substance of this form is derived from cosmic matter or star matter, roughly speaking. But the old Sanskrit word describes it exactly — *Linga Sarira*, the design body — because it is the design or model for the physical body. This is better than "ethereal body," as the latter might be said to be subsequent to the physical, whereas in fact the astral body precedes the material one.

The astral body is made of matter of very fine texture as compared with the visible body, and has a great tensile strength, so that it changes but little during a lifetime, while the physical alters every moment. And not only has it this immense strength, but at the same time possesses an elasticity permitting its extension to a considerable distance. It is flexible, plastic, extensible, and strong. The matter of which it is composed is electrical and magnetic in its essence, and is just what the whole world was composed of in the dim past when the processes of evolution had not yet arrived at the point of producing the material body for man. But it is not raw or crude matter. Having been through a vast period of evolution and undergone purifying processes of an incalculable number, its nature has been refined to a degree far beyond the gross physical elements we see and touch with the physical eye and hand.

The astral body is the guiding model for the physical one, and all the other kingdoms have the same astral model. Vegetables, minerals, and animals have the ethereal double, and this theory is the only one which will answer the question how it is that the seed produces its own kind and all sentient beings bring forth their like. Biologists can only say that the facts are as we know them, but can give no reason why the acorn will never grow anything but an oak except that no man ever knew it to be otherwise. But in the old schools of the past the true doctrine was known, and it has been once again brought out in the West through the efforts of H. P. Blavatsky and those who have found inspiration in her works.

This doctrine is, that in early times of the evolution of this globe the various kingdoms of nature are outlined in plan or ideal form first, and then the astral matter begins to work on this plan with the aid of the Life principle, until after long ages the astral human form is evolved and perfected. This is, then, the first form that the human race had, and corresponds in a way with the allegory of man's state in the garden of Eden. After another long period, during which the cycle of further descent into matter is rolling forward, the astral form at last clothes itself with a "coat of skin," and the present physical form is on the scene. This is the explanation of the verse of the book of Genesis which describes the giving of coats of skin to Adam and Eve. It is the final fall into matter, for from that point on the man within strives to raise the whole mass of physical substance up to a higher level, and to inform it all with a larger measure of spiritual influence, so that it may be ready to go still further on during the next great period of evolution after the present one is ended. So at the present time the model for the growing child in the womb is the astral body already perfect in shape before the child is born. It is on this the molecules arrange themselves until the child is complete, and the presence of the ethereal design-body will explain how the form grows into shape, how the eyes push themselves out from within to the surface of the face, and many other mysterious matters in embryology which are passed over by medical men with a description but with no explanation. This will also explain, as nothing else can, the cases of marking of the child in the womb sometimes denied by physicians but well-known by those who care to watch, to be a fact of frequent occurrence. The growing physical form is subject to the astral model; it is connected with the imagination of the mother by physical and psychical organs; the mother makes a strong picture from horror, fear, or otherwise, and the astral model is then similarly affected. In the case of marking by being born legless, the ideas and strong imagination of the mother act so as to cut off or shrivel up the astral leg, and the result is that the molecules, having no model of leg to work on, make no physical leg whatever; and similarly in all such cases. But where we find a man who still feels the leg which the surgeon has cut off, or perceives the fingers that were amputated, then the astral member has not been interfered with, and hence the man feels as if it were still on his person. For knife or acid will not injure the astral model, but in the first stages of its growth ideas and imagination have the power of acid and sharpened steel.

In the ordinary man who has not been trained in practical occultism or who has not the faculty by birth, the astral body cannot go more than a few feet from the physical one. It is a part of that physical, it sustains it and is incorporated in it just as the fibers of the mango are all through that fruit. But there are those who, by reason of practices pursued in former lives on the earth, have a power born with them of unconsciously sending out the astral body. These are mediums, some seers, and many hysterical, cataleptic, and scrofulous people. Those who have trained themselves by a long course of excessively hard discipline which reaches to the moral and mental nature and quite beyond the power of the average man of the day, can use the astral form at will, for they have gotten completely over the delusion that the physical body is a permanent part of them, and, besides, they have learned the chemical and electrical laws governing in this matter. In their case they act with knowledge and consciously; in the other cases the act is done without power to prevent it, or to bring it about at will, or to avoid the risks attendant on such use of potencies in nature of a high character.

The astral body has in it the real organs of the outer sense organs. In it are the sight, hearing, power to smell, and the sense of touch. It has a complete system of nerves and arteries of its own for the conveyance of the astral fluid which is to that body as our blood is to the physical. It is the real personal man. There are located the subconscious perception and the latent memory, which the hypnotizers of the day are dealing with and being baffled by. So when the body dies the astral man is released, and as at death the immortal man — the Triad — flies away to another state, the astral becomes a shell of the once living man and requires time to dissipate. It retains all the memories of the life lived by the man, and thus reflexly and automatically can repeat what the dead man knew, said, thought, and saw. It remains near the deserted physical body nearly all the time until that is completely dissipated, for it has to go through its own process of dying. It may become visible under certain conditions. It is the spook of the spiritualistic séance-rooms, and is there made to masquerade as the real spirit of this or that individual. Attracted by the thoughts of the medium and the sitters, it vaguely flutters where they are, and then is galvanized into a factitious life by a whole host of elemental forces and by the active astral body of the medium who is holding the séance or of any other medium in the audience. From it (as from a photograph) are then reflected into the medium's brain all the boasted evidences which spiritualists claim go to prove identity of deceased friend or relative. These evidences are accepted as proof that the spirit of the deceased is present, because neither mediums nor sitters are acquainted with the laws governing their own nature, nor with the constitution, power, and function of astral matter and astral man.

The Theosophical philosophy does not deny the facts proven in spiritualistic séances, but it gives an explanation of them wholly opposed to that of the spiritualists. And surely the utter absence of any logical scientific explanation by these so-called spirits of the phenomena they are said to produce supports the contention that they have no knowledge to impart. They can merely cause certain phenomena; the examination of those and deductions therefrom can only be properly carried on by a trained brain guided by a living trinity of spirit, soul, and mind. And here another class of spiritualistic phenomena requires brief notice. That is the appearance of what is called a "materialized spirit."

Three explanations are offered: *First,* that the astral body of the living medium detaches itself from its corpus and assumes the appearance of the so-called spirit; for one of the properties of the astral matter is capacity to reflect an image existing unseen in ether. *Second,* the actual astral shell of the deceased — wholly devoid of his or her spirit and conscience — becomes visible and tangible when the condition of air and ether is such as to so alter the vibration of the molecules of the astral shell that it may become visible. The phenomena of density and apparent weight are explained by other laws. *Third,* an unseen mass of electrical and magnetic matter is collected, and upon it is reflected out of the astral light a picture of any desired person either dead or living. This is taken to be the "spirit" of such persons, but it is not, and has been justly called by H. P. Blavatsky a "psychological fraud," because it pretends to be what it is not. And, strange to say, this very explanation of materializations has been given by a "spirit" at a regular séance, but has never been accepted by the spiritualists just because it upsets their notion of the return of the spirits of deceased persons.

Finally, the astral body will explain nearly all the strange psychical things happening in daily life and in dealings with genuine mediums; it shows what an apparition may be and the possibility of such being seen, and thus prevents the scientific doubter from violating good sense by asserting you did not see what you know you have seen; it removes superstition by showing the real nature of these phenomena, and destroys the unreasonable fear of the unknown which makes a man afraid to see a "ghost." By it also we can explain the apportation of objects without physical contact, for the astral hand may be extruded and made to take hold of an object, drawing it in toward the body. When this is shown to be possible, then travelers will not be laughed at who tell of seeing the Hindu yogee make coffee cups fly through the air and distant objects approach apparently of their own accord untouched by him or anyone else. All the instances of clairvoyance and clairaudience are to be explained also by the astral body and astral light. The astral — which are the real — organs do the seeing and the hearing, and as all material objects are constantly in motion among their own atoms the astral sight and hearing are not impeded, but work at a distance as great as the extension of the astral light or matter around and about the earth. Thus it was that the great seer Swedenborg saw houses burning in the city of Stockholm when he was at another city many miles off, and by the same means any clairvoyant of the day sees and hears at a distance.

CHAPTER VI
Kama — Desire

THE author of *Esoteric Buddhism* — which book ought to be consulted by all students of Theosophy, since it was made from suggestions given by some of the Adepts themselves — gave the name *Kama rupa* to the fourth principle of man's constitution. The reason was that the word *Kama* in the Sanskrit language means "desire," and as the idea intended to be conveyed was that the fourth principle was the "body or mass of desires and passions," Mr. Sinnett added the Sanskrit word for body or form, which is *Rupa,* thus making the compound word *Kamarupa.* I shall call it by the English equivalent — passions and desires — because those terms exactly express its nature. And I do this also in order to make the sharp issue which actually exists between the psychology and mental philosophy of the west and those of the east. The west divides man into intellect, will, and feeling, but it is not understood whether the passions and desires constitute a principle in themselves or are due entirely to the body. Indeed, most people consider them as being the result of the influence of the flesh, for they are designated often by the terms "desires of the flesh" and "fleshly appetites." The ancients, however, and the Theosophists know them to be a principle in themselves and not merely the impulses from the body. There is no help to be had in this matter from the western psychology, now in its infancy and wholly devoid of knowledge about the inner, which is the psychical, nature of man, and from this point there is the greatest divergence between it and Theosophy.

The passions and desires are not produced by the body, but, on the contrary, the body is caused to be by the former. It is desire and passion which caused us to be born, and will bring us to birth again and again in this body or in some other.* It is by passion and desire we are made to evolve through the mansions of death called lives on earth. It was by the arising of desire in the unknown first cause, the one absolute existence, that the whole collection of worlds was manifested, and by means of the influence of desire in the now manifested world is the latter kept in existence.

This fourth principle is the balance principle of the whole seven. It stands in the middle, and from it the ways go up or down. It is the basis of action and the mover of the will. As the old Hermetists say: "Behind will stands desire." For whether we wish to do well or ill we have to first arouse within us the desire for either course. The good man who at last becomes even a sage had at one time in his many lives to arouse the desire for the company of holy men and to keep his desire for progress alive in order to continue on his way. Even a Buddha or a Jesus had first to make a vow, which is a desire, in some life, that he would save the world or some part of it, and to persevere with the desire alive in his heart through countless lives. And equally so, on the other hand, the bad man life after life took unto himself low, selfish, wicked desires, thus debasing instead of purifying this principle. On the material

*[In *The Theosophical Forum*, June, 1894, page 12, Judge corrected this to: "in some body on this earth or another globe."]

and scientific side of occultism, the use of the inner hidden powers of our nature, if this principle of desire be not strong the master power of imagination cannot do its work, because though it makes a mold or matrix the will cannot act unless it is moved, directed, and kept up to pitch by desire.

The desires and passions, therefore, have two aspects, the one being low and the other high. The low is that shown by the constant placing of the consciousness entirely below in the body and the astral body; the high comes from the influence of and aspiration to the trinity above, of Mind, Buddhi, and Spirit. This fourth principle is like the sign Libra in the path of the Sun through the Zodiac; when the Sun (who is the real man) reaches that sign he trembles in the balance. Should he go back, the worlds would be destroyed; he goes onward, and the whole human race is lifted up to perfection.

During life the emplacement of the desires and passions is, as obtains with the astral body, throughout the entire lower man, and like that ethereal counterpart of our physical person it may be added to or diminished, made weak or increased in strength, debased or purified.

At death it informs the astral body, which then becomes a mere shell; for when a man dies his astral body and principle of passion and desire leave the physical in company and coalesce. It is then that the term *Kamarupa* may be applied, as *Kamarupa* is really made of astral body and *Kama* in conjunction, and this joining of the two makes a shape or form which though ordinarily invisible is material and may be brought into visibility. Although it is empty of mind and conscience, it has powers of its own that can be exercised whenever the conditions permit.

CHAPTER VI

These conditions are furnished by the medium of the spiritualists, and in every *séance* room the astral shells of deceased persons are always present to delude the sitters, whose powers of discrimination have been destroyed by wonderment. It is the "devil" of the Hindus, and a worse enemy the poor medium could not have. For the astral spook — or *Kamarupa* — is but the mass of the desires and passions abandoned by the real person who has fled to "heaven" and has no concern with the people left behind, least of all with *séances* and mediums. Hence, being devoid of the nobler soul, these desires and passions work only on the very lowest part of the medium's nature and stir up no good elements, but always the lower leanings of the being. Therefore it is that even the spiritualists themselves admit that in the ranks of the mediums there is much fraud, and mediums have often confessed, "the spirits did tempt me and I committed fraud at their wish."

This *Kamarupa* spook is also the enemy of our civilization, which permits us to execute men for crimes committed and thus throw out into the ether the mass of passion and desire free from the weight of the body and liable at any moment to be attracted to any sensitive person. Being thus attracted, the deplorable images of crimes committed and also the picture of the execution and all the accompanying curses and wishes for revenge are implanted in living persons, who, not seeing the evil, are unable to throw it off. Thus crimes and new ideas of crimes are wilfully propagated every day by those countries where capital punishment prevails.

The astral shells together with the still living astral body of the medium, helped by certain forces of nature which the Theosophists call "elementals," produce nearly all the phenomena of non-fraudulent spiritualism. The medium's astral body having the power of extension and extrusion forms the framework for what are called "materialized spirits," makes objects move without physical contact, gives reports from deceased relatives, none of them anything more than recollections and pictures from the astral light, and in all this using and being used by the shells of suicides, executed murderers, and all such spooks as are naturally near to this plane of life. The number of cases in which any communication comes from an actual spirit out of the body is so small as to be countable almost on one hand. But the spirits of living men sometimes, while their bodies are asleep, come to *séances* and take part therein. But they cannot recollect it, do not know how they do it, and are not distinguished by mediums from the mass of astral corpses. The fact that such things can be done by the inner man and not be recollected proves nothing against these theories, for the child can see without knowing how the eye acts, and the savage who has no knowledge of the complex machinery working in his body still carries on the process of digestion perfectly. And that the latter is unconscious with him is exactly in line with the theory, for these acts and doings of the inner man are the unconscious actions of the subconscious mind. These words "conscious" and "subconscious" are of course used relatively, the unconsciousness being that of the brain only. And hypnotic experiments have conclusively proved all these theories, as on one day not far away will be fully admitted. Besides this, the astral shells of suicides and executed criminals are the most coherent, longest lived, and nearest to us of all the shades of hades, and hence must, out of the necessity of the case, be the real "controls" of the *séance* room.

Passion and desire together with astral model-body are common to men and animals, as also to the vegetable kingdom, though in the last but faintly developed. And at one period in evolution no further material principles had been developed, and all the three higher, of Mind, Soul, and Spirit, were but latent. Up to this point man and animal were equal, for the brute in us is made of the passions and the astral body. The development of the germs of Mind made man because it constituted the great differentiation. The God within begins with *Manas* or mind, and it is the struggle between this God and the brute below which Theosophy speaks of and warns about. The lower principle is called bad because by comparison with the higher it is so, but still it is the basis of action. We cannot rise unless self first asserts itself in the desire to do better. In this aspect it is called *rajas* or the active and bad quality, as distinguished from *tamas,* or the quality of darkness and indifference. Rising is not possible unless *rajas* is present to give the impulse, and by the use of this principle of passion all the higher qualities are brought to at last so refine and elevate our desires that they may be continually placed upon truth and spirit. By this Theosophy does not teach that the passions are to be pandered to or satiated, for a more pernicious doctrine was never taught, but the injunction is to make use of the activity given by the fourth principle so as to ever rise and not to fall under the dominion of the dark quality that ends with annihilation, after having begun in selfishness and indifference.

CHAPTER VI

Having thus gone over the field and shown what are the lower principles, we find Theosophy teaching that at the present point of man's evolution he is a fully developed quaternary with the higher principles partly developed. Hence it is taught that today man shows himself to be moved by passion and desire. This is proved by a glance at the civilizations of the earth, for they are all moved by this principle, and in countries like France, England, and America a glorification of it is exhibited in the attention to display, to sensuous art, to struggle for power and place, and in all the habits and modes of living where the gratification of the senses is sometimes esteemed the highest good. But as Mind is being evolved more and more as we proceed in our course along the line of the race development, there can be perceived underneath in all countries the beginning of the transition from the animal possessed of the germ of real mind to the man of mind complete. This day is therefore known to the Masters, who have given out some of the old truths, as the "transition period." Proud science and prouder religion do not admit this, but think we are as we always will be. But believing in his teacher, the theosophist sees all around him the evidence that the race mind is changing by enlargement, that the old days of dogmatism are gone and the "age of inquiry" has come, that the inquiries will grow louder year by year and the answers be required to satisfy the mind as it grows more and more, until at last, all dogmatism being ended, the race will be ready to face all problems, each man for himself, all working for the good of the whole, and that the end will be the perfecting of those who struggle to overcome the brute. For these reasons the old doctrines are given out again, and Theosophy asks every one to reflect whether to give way to the animal below or look up to and be governed by the God within.

A fuller treatment of the fourth principle of our constitution would compel us to consider all such questions as those presented by the wonder workers of the east, by spiritualistic phenomena, hypnotism, apparitions, insanity, and the like, but they must be reserved for separate handling.

CHAPTER VII
Manas

In our analysis of man's nature we have so far considered only the perishable elements which make up the lower man, and have arrived at the fourth principle or plane — that of desire — without having touched upon the question of Mind. But even so far as we have gone it must be evident that there is a wide difference between the ordinary ideas about Mind and those found in Theosophy. Ordinarily the Mind is thought to be immaterial, or to be merely the name for the action of the brain in evolving thought, a process wholly unknown other than by inference, or that if there be no brain there can be no mind. A good deal of attention has been paid to cataloguing some mental functions and attributes, but the terms are altogether absent from the language to describe actual metaphysical and spiritual facts about man. This confusion and poverty of words for these uses are due almost entirely, first, to dogmatic religion, which has asserted and enforced for many centuries dogmas and doctrines which reason could not accept, and secondly to the natural war which grew up between science and religion just as soon as the fetters placed by religion upon science were removed and the latter was permitted to deal with facts in nature. The reaction against religion naturally prevented science from taking any but a materialistic view of man and nature. So from neither of these two have we yet gained the words needed for describing the fifth, sixth, and seventh principles, those which make up the Trinity, the real man, the immortal pilgrim.

The fifth principle is *Manas,* in the classification adopted by Mr. Sinnett, and is usually translated Mind. Other names have been given to it, but it is the knower, the perceiver, the thinker. The sixth is *Buddhi,* or spiritual discernment; the seventh is *Atma,* or Spirit, the ray from the Absolute Being. The English language will suffice to describe in part what *Manas* is, but not *Buddhi,* or *Atma,* and will leave many things relating to *Manas* undescribed.

The course of evolution developed the lower principles and produced at last the form of man with a brain of better and deeper capacity than that of any other animal. But this man in form was not man in mind, and needed the fifth principle, the thinking, perceiving one, to differentiate him from the animal kingdom and to confer the power of becoming self-conscious. The monad was imprisoned in these forms, and that monad is composed of *Atma* and *Buddhi;* for without the presence of the monad evolution could not go forward. Going back for a moment to the time when the races were devoid of mind, the question arises, "who gave the mind, where did it come from, and what is it?" It is the link between the Spirit of God above and the personal below; it was given to the mindless monads by others who had gone all through this process ages upon ages before in other worlds and systems of worlds, and it therefore came from other evolutionary periods which were carried out and completed long before the solar system had begun. This is the theory, strange and unacceptable today, but which must be stated if we are to tell the truth about theosophy; and this is only handing on what others have said before.

The manner in which this light of mind was given to

the Mindless Men can be understood from the illustration of one candle lighting many. Given one lighted candle and numerous unlighted ones, it follows that from one light the others may also be set aflame. So in the case of *Manas.* It is the candle of flame. The mindless men having four elementary principles of Body, Astral Body, Life and Desire, are the unlighted candles that cannot light themselves. The Sons of Wisdom, who are the Elder Brothers of every family of men on any globe, have the light, derived by them from others who reach back, and yet farther back, in endless procession with no beginning or end. They set fire to the combined lower principles and the Monad, thus lighting up *Manas* in the new men and preparing another great race for final initiation. This lighting up of the fire of *Manas* is symbolized in all great religions and Freemasonry. In the east one priest appears holding a candle lighted at the altar, and thousands of others light their candles from this one. The Parsees also have their sacred fire which is lighted from some other sacred flame.

Manas, or the Thinker, is the reincarnating being, the immortal who carries the results and values of all the different lives lived on earth or elsewhere. Its nature becomes dual as soon as it is attached to a body. For the human brain is a superior organism and *Manas* uses it to reason from premises to conclusions. This also differentiates man from animal, for the animal acts from automatic and so-called instinctual impulses, whereas the man can use reason. This is the lower aspect of the Thinker or *Manas,* and not, as some have supposed, the highest and best gift belonging to man. Its other, and in theosophy higher, aspect is the intuitional, which knows, and does not depend on reason. The lower, and purely intellectual, is nearest to the principle of Desire, and is thus distinguished from its other side which has affinity for the spiritual principles above. If the Thinker, then, becomes wholly intellectual, the entire nature begins to tend downward; for intellect alone is cold, heartless, selfish, because it is not lighted up by the two other principles of *Buddhi* and *Atma.*

In *Manas* the thoughts of all lives are stored. That is to say: in any one life, the sum total of thoughts underlying all the acts of the life-time will be of one character in general, but may be placed in one or more classes. That is, the business man of today is a single type; his entire life thoughts represent but one single thread of thought. The artist is another. The man who has engaged in business, but also thought much upon fame and power which he never attained, is still another. The great mass of self-sacrificing, courageous, and strong poor people who have but little time to think, constitute another distinct class. In all these the total quantity of life thoughts makes up the stream or thread of a life's meditation — "that upon which the heart was set" — and is stored in *Manas,* to be brought out again at any time in whatever life the brain and bodily environments are similar to those used in engendering that class of thoughts.

It is *Manas* which sees the objects presented to it by the bodily organs and the actual organs within. When the open eye receives a picture on the retina, the whole scene is turned into vibrations in the optic nerves which disappear into the brain, where *Manas* is enabled to perceive them as idea. And so with every other organ or sense. If the connection between *Manas* and the brain be broken, intelligence will not be manifested unless *Manas* has by training found out how to project the astral body from the physical and thereby keep up communication with fellowmen. That the organs and senses do not cognize objects, hypnotism, mesmerism, and spiritualism have now proved. For, as we see in mesmeric and hypnotic experiments, the object seen or felt, and from which all the effects of solid objects may be sensed, is often only an idea existing in the operator's brain. In the same way *Manas,* using the astral body, has only to impress an idea upon the other person to make the latter see the idea and translate it into a visible body from which the usual effects of density and weight seem to follow. And in hypnotism there are many experiments, all of which go to show that so called matter is not *per se* solid or dense; that sight does not always depend on the eye and rays of light proceeding from an object; that the intangible for one normal brain and organs may be perfectly tangible for another; and that physical effects in the body may be produced from an idea solely. The well-known experiments of producing a blister by a simple piece of paper, or preventing a real blistering plaster from making a blister, by force of the idea conveyed to a subject, either that there was to be or not to be a blister, conclusively prove the power of effecting an impulse on matter by the use of that which is called *Manas.* But all these phenomena are the exhibition of the powers of lower *Manas* acting in the astral Body and the fourth principle — Desire, using the physical body as the field for the exhibition of the forces.

It is this lower *Manas* which retains all the impressions of a life-time and sometimes strangely exhibits them in trances or dreams, delirium, induced states, here and there in normal conditions, and very often at the time of physical death. But it is so occupied with the brain, with memory and with sensation, that it usually presents but few recollections out of the mass of events that years have brought before it. It interferes with the action of Higher *Manas* because just at the present point of evolution, Desire and all corresponding powers, faculties, and senses are the most highly developed, thus obscuring, as it were, the white light of the spiritual side of *Manas.* It is tinted by each object presented to it, whether it be a thought-object or a material one. That is to say, Lower *Manas* operating through the brain is at once altered into the shape and other characteristics of any object, mental or otherwise. This causes it to have four peculiarities. *First,* to naturally fly off from any point, object, or subject; *second,* to fly to some pleasant idea; *third,* to fly to an unpleasant idea; *fourth,* to remain passive and considering naught. The first is due to memory and the natural motion of *Manas*; the second and third are due to memory alone; the fourth signifies sleep when not abnormal, and when abnormal is going toward insanity. These mental characteristics all belonging to Lower *Manas,* are those which the Higher *Manas,* aided by *Buddhi* and *Atma,* has to fight and conquer. Higher *Manas,* if able to act, becomes what we sometimes call Genius; if completely master, then one may become a god. But memory continually presents pictures to Lower *Manas,* and the result is that the Higher is obscured. Sometimes, however, along the pathway of life we do see here and there men who are geniuses or great seers and prophets. In these the Higher powers of *Manas* are active and the person illuminated. Such were the great Sages of the past, men like Buddha, Jesus, Confucius, Zoroaster, and others. Poets, too, such as Tennyson, Longfellow, and others, are men in whom Higher *Manas* now and then sheds a bright ray on the man below, to be soon obscured, however, by the effect of dogmatic religious education which has given memory certain pictures that always prevent *Manas* from gaining full activity.

In this higher Trinity, we have the God above each one; this is *Atma,* and may be called the Higher Self.

Next is the spiritual part of the soul called *Buddhi;* when thoroughly united with *Manas* this may be called the Divine Ego.

The inner Ego, who reincarnates, taking on body after body, storing up the impressions of life after life, gaining experience and adding it to the divine Ego, suffering and enjoying through an immense period of years, is the fifth principle — *Manas* — not united to *Buddhi.* This is the permanent individuality which gives to every man the feeling of being himself and not some other; that which through all the changes of the days and nights from youth to the end of life makes us feel one identity through all the period; it bridges the gap made by sleep; in like manner it bridges the gap made by the sleep of death. It is this, and not our brain, that lifts us above the animal. The depth and variety of the brain convolutions in man are caused by the presence of *Manas,* and are not the cause of mind. And when we either wholly or now and then become consciously united with *Buddhi,* the Spiritual Soul, we behold God, as it were. This is what the ancients all desired to see, but what the moderns do not believe in, the latter preferring rather to throw away their own right to be great in nature, and to worship an imaginary god made up solely of their own fancies and not very different from weak human nature.

This permanent individuality in the present race has therefore been through every sort of experience, for Theosophy insists on its permanence and in the necessity for its continuing to take part in evolution. It has a duty to perform, consisting in raising up to a higher state all the matter concerned in the chain of globes to which the earth belongs. We have all lived and taken part in civilization after civilization, race after race, on earth, and will so continue throughout all the rounds and races until the seventh is complete. At the same time it should be remembered that the matter of this globe and that connected with it has also been through every kind of form, with possibly some exceptions in very low planes of mineral formation. But in general all the matter visible, or held in space still unprecipitated, has been molded at one time or another into forms of all varieties, many of these being such as we now have no idea of. The processes of evolution, therefore, in some departments, now go forward with greater rapidity than in former ages because both *Manas* and matter have acquired facility of action. Especially is this so in regard to man, who is the farthest ahead of all things or beings in this evolution. He is now incarnated and projected into life more quickly than in earlier periods when it consumed many years to obtain a "coat of skin." This coming into life over and over again cannot be avoided by the ordinary man because Lower *Manas* is still bound by Desire, which is the preponderating principle at the present period. Being so influenced by Desire *Manas* is continually deluded while in the body, and being thus deluded is unable to prevent the action upon it of the forces set up in the life time. These forces are generated by *Manas,* that is, by the thinking of the life time. Each thought makes a physical as well as mental link with the desire in which it is rooted. All life is filled with such thoughts, and when the period of rest after death is ended *Manas* is bound by innumerable electrical magnetic threads to earth by reason of the thoughts of the last life, and therefore by desire, for it was desire that caused so many thoughts and ignorance of the true nature of things. An understanding of this doctrine of man being really a thinker and made of thought will make clear all the rest in relation to incarnation and reincarnation. The body of the inner man is made of thought, and this being so it must follow that if the thoughts have more affinity for earth-life than for life elsewhere a return to life here is inevitable.

At the present day *Manas* is not fully active in the race, as Desire still is uppermost. In the next cycle of the human period *Manas* will be fully active and developed in the entire race. Hence the people of the earth have not yet come to the point of making a conscious choice as to the path they will take; but when in the cycle referred to, *Manas* is active, all will then be compelled to consciously make the choice to right or left, the one leading to complete and conscious union with *Atma,* the other to the annihilation of those beings who prefer that path.

CHAPTER VII

CHAPTER VIII
Of Reincarnation

How man has come to be the complex being that he is and why, are questions that neither Science nor Religion makes conclusive answer to. This immortal thinker having such vast powers and possibilities, all his because of his intimate connection with every secret part of Nature from which he has been built up, stands at the top of an immense and silent evolution. He asks why Nature exists, what the drama of life has for its aim, how that aim may be attained. But Science and Religion both fail to give a reasonable reply. Science does not pretend to be able to give the solution, saying that the examination of things as they are is enough of a task; religion offers an explanation both illogical and unmeaning and acceptable but to the bigot, as it requires us to consider the whole of Nature as a mystery and to seek for the meaning and purpose of life with all its sorrow in the pleasure of a God who cannot be found out. The educated and enquiring mind knows that dogmatic religion can only give an answer invented by man while it pretends to be from God.

What then is the universe for, and for what final purpose is man the immortal thinker here in evolution? It is all for the experience and emancipation of the soul, for the purpose of raising the entire mass of manifested matter up to the stature, nature, and dignity of conscious god-hood. The great aim is to reach self-consciousness; not through a race or a tribe or some favored nation, but by and through the perfecting, after transformation, of the whole mass of matter as well as what we now call soul. Nothing is or is to be left out. The aim for present man is his initiation into complete knowledge, and for the other kingdoms below him that they may be raised up gradually from stage to stage to be in time initiated also. This is evolution carried to its highest power; it is a magnificent prospect; it makes of man a god, and gives to every part of nature the possibility of being one day the same; there is strength and nobility in it, for by this no man is dwarfed and belittled, for no one is so originally sinful that he cannot rise above all sin. Treated from the materialistic position of Science, evolution takes in but half of life; while the religious conception of it is a mixture of nonsense and fear. Present religions keep the element of fear, and at the same time imagine that an Almighty being can think of no other earth but this and has to govern this one very imperfectly. But the old theosophical view makes the universe a vast, complete, and perfect whole.

Now the moment we postulate a double evolution, physical and spiritual, we have at the same time to admit that it can only be carried on by reincarnation. This is, in fact, demonstrated by science. It is shown that the matter of the earth and of all things physical upon it was at one time either gaseous or molten; that it cooled; that it altered; that from its alterations and evolutions at last were produced all the great variety of things and beings. This, on the physical plane, is transformation or change from one form to another. The total mass of matter is about the same as in the beginning of this globe, with a very minute allowance for some star dust. Hence it must have been changed over and over again, and thus been physically reformed and reembodied. Of course, to be strictly accurate, we cannot use the word reincarnation, because "incarnate" refers to flesh. Let us say "reembodied," and then we see that both for matter and for man there has been a constant change of form and this is, broadly speaking, "reincarnation." As to the whole mass of matter, the doctrine is that it will all be raised to man's estate when man has gone further on himself. There is no residuum left after man's final salvation which in a mysterious way is to be disposed of or done away with in some remote dust-heap of nature. The true doctrine allows for nothing like that, and at the same time is not afraid to give the true disposition of what would seem to be a residuum. It is all worked up into other states, for as the philosophy declares there is no inorganic matter whatever but that every atom is alive and has the germ of self-consciousness, it must follow that one day it will all have been changed. Thus what is now called human flesh is so much matter that one day was wholly mineral, later on vegetable, and now refined into human atoms. At a point of time very far from now the present vegetable matter will have been raised to the animal stage and what we now use as our organic or fleshy matter will have changed by transformation through evolution into self-conscious thinkers, and so on up the whole scale until the time shall come when what is now known as mineral matter will have passed on to the human stage and out into that of thinker. Then at the coming on of another great period of evolution the mineral matter of that time will be some which is now passing through its lower transformations on other planets and in other systems of worlds. This is perhaps a "fanciful" scheme for the men of the present day, who are so accustomed to being called bad, sinful, weak, and utterly foolish from their birth that they fear to believe the truth about themselves, but for the disciples of the ancient theosophists it is not impossible or fanciful, but is logical and vast. And no doubt it will one day be admitted by everyone when the mind of the western race has broken away from Mosaic chronology and Mosaic ideas of men and nature. Therefore as to reincarnation and metempsychosis we say that they are first to be applied to the whole cosmos and not alone to man. But as man is the most interesting object to himself, we will consider in detail its application to him.

This is the most ancient of doctrines and is believed in now by more human minds than the number of those who do not hold it. The millions in the East almost all accept it; it was taught by the Greeks; a large number of the Chinese now believe it as their forefathers did before them; the Jews thought it was true, and it has not disappeared from their religion; and Jesus, who is called the founder of Christianity, also believed and taught it. In the early Christian church it was known and taught, and the very best of the fathers of the church believed and promulgated it.

Christians should remember that Jesus was a Jew who thought his mission was to Jews, for he says in St. Matthew, "I am not sent but unto the lost sheep of the house of Israel." He must have well known the doctrines held by them. They all believed in reincarnation. For them Moses, Adam, Noah, Seth, and others had returned to earth, and at the time of Jesus it was currently believed that the old prophet Elias was yet to return. So we find, first, that Jesus never denied the doctrine, and on various occasions assented to it, as when he said that John the Baptist was actually the Elias of old whom the people were expecting. All this can be seen by consulting St. Matthew in chapters xvii, xi, and others.

In these it is very clear that Jesus is shown as approving the doctrine of reincarnation. And following Jesus we find St. Paul, in Romans ix, speaking of Esau and Jacob being actually in existence before they were born, and later such great Christian fathers as Origen, Synesius, and others believing and teaching the theory. In Proverbs viii, 22, we have Solomon saying that when the earth was made he was present, and that, long before he could have been born as Solomon, his delights were in the habitable parts of the earth with the sons of men. St. John the Revelator says in Revs. iii, 12, he was told in a vision which refers to the voice of God or the voice of one speaking for God, that whosoever should overcome would not be under the necessity of "going out" any more, that is, would not need to be reincarnated. For five hundred years after Jesus the doctrine was taught in the church until the council of Constantinople. Then a condemnation was passed upon a phase of the question which has been regarded by many as against reincarnation, but if that condemnation goes against the words of Jesus it is of no effect. It does go against him, and thus the church is in the position of saying in effect that Jesus did not know enough to curse, as it did, a doctrine known and taught in his day and which was brought to his notice prominently and never condemned but in fact approved by him. Christianity is a Jewish religion, and this doctrine of reincarnation belongs to it historically by succession from the Jews, and also by reason of its having been taught by Jesus and the early fathers of the church. If there be any truthful or logical way for the Christian church to get out of this position — excluding, of course, dogmas of the church — the theosophist would like to be shown it. Indeed, the theosophist holds that whenever a professed Christian denies the theory he thereby sets up his judgment against that of Jesus, who must have known more about the matter than those who follow him. It is the anathema hurled by the church council and the absence of the doctrine from the teaching now that have damaged Christianity and made of all the Christian nations people who pretend to be followers of Jesus and the law of love, but who really as nations are followers of the Mosaic law of retaliation. For alone in reincarnation is the answer to all the problems of life, and in it and Karma is the force that will make men pursue in fact the ethics they have in theory. It is the aim of the old philosophy to restore this doctrine to whatsoever religion has lost it; and hence we call it the "lost chord of Christianity."

But who or what is it that reincarnates? It is not the body, for that dies and disintegrates; and but few of us would like to be chained forever to such bodies as we now have, admitted to be infected with disease except in the case of the savage. It is not the astral body, for, as shown, that also has its term and must go to pieces after the physical has gone. Nor is it the passions and desires. They, to be sure, have a very long term, because they have the power to reproduce themselves in each life so long as we do not eradicate them. And reincarnation provides for that, since we are given by it many opportunities of slowly, one by one, killing off the desires and passions which mar the heavenly picture of the spiritual man.

It has been shown how the passional part of us coalesces with the astral after death and makes a seeming being that has a short life to live while it is disintegrating. When the separation is complete between the body that has died, the astral body, and the passions and desires — life having begun to busy itself with other forms — the Higher Triad, *Manas, Buddhi*, and *Atma,* who are the real man, immediately go into another state, and when that state, which is called *Devachan,* or heaven, is over, they are attracted back to earth for reincarnation. They are the immortal part of us; they, in fact, and no other are we. This should be firmly grasped by the mind, for upon its clear understanding depends the comprehension of the entire doctrine. What stands in the way of the modern western man's seeing this clearly is the long training we have all had in materialistic science and materializing religion, both of which have made the mere physical body too prominent. The one has taught of matter alone and the other has preached the resurrection of the body, a doctrine against common sense, fact, logic, and testimony. But there is no doubt that the theory of the bodily resurrection has arisen from the corruption of the older and true teaching. Resurrection is founded on what Job says about seeing his redeemer in his flesh, and on St. Paul's remark that the body was raised incorruptible. But Job was an Egyptian who spoke of seeing his teacher or initiator, who was the redeemer, and Jesus and Paul referred to the spiritual body only.

Although reincarnation is the law of nature, the complete trinity of *Atma-Buddhi-Manas* does not yet fully incarnate in this race. They use and occupy the body by means of the entrance of *Manas,* the lowest of the three, and the other two shine upon it from above, constituting the God in Heaven. This was symbolized in the old Jewish teaching about the Heavenly Man who stands with his head in heaven and his feet in hell. That is, the head *Atma* and *Buddhi* are yet in heaven, and the feet, *Manas,* walk in hell, which is the body and physical life. For that reason man is not yet fully conscious, and reincarnations are needed to at last complete the incarnation of the whole trinity in the body. When that has been accomplished the race will have become as gods, and the godlike trinity being in full possession the entire mass of matter will be perfected and raised up for the next step. This is the real meaning of "the word made flesh." It was so grand a thing in the case of any single person, such as Jesus or Buddha, as to be looked upon as a divine incarnation. And out of this, too, comes the idea of the crucifixion, for *Manas* is thus crucified for the purpose of raising up the thief to paradise.

It is because the trinity is not yet incarnate in the race that life has so many mysteries, some of which are showing themselves from day to day in all the various experiments made on and in man.

The physician knows not what life is nor why the body moves as it does, because the spiritual portion is yet enshrouded in the clouds of heaven; the scientist is wandering in the dark, confounded and confused by all that hypnotism and other strange things bring before him, because the conscious man is out of sight on the very top of the divine mountain, thus compelling the learned to speak of the "subconscious mind," the "latent personality," and the like; and the priest can give us no light at all because he denies man's god-like nature, reduces all to the level of original sin, and puts upon our conception of God the black mark of inability to control or manage the creation without invention of expedients to cure supposed errors. But this old truth solves the riddle and paints God and Nature in harmonious colors.

Reincarnation does not mean that we go into animal forms after death, as is believed by some Eastern peoples. "Once a man always a man" is the saying in the Great Lodge. But it would not be too much punishment for some men were it possible to condemn them to rebirth in brute bodies; however nature does not go by sentiment but by law, and we, not being able to see all, cannot say that the brutal man is brute all through his nature. And evolution having brought *Manas* the Thinker and Immortal Person on to this plane, cannot send him back to the brute which has not *Manas.*

By looking into two explanations for the literal acceptation by some people in the East of those laws of Manu which seem to teach the transmigrating into brutes, insects, and so on, we can see how the true student of this doctrine will not fall into the same error.

The first is, that the various verses and books teaching such transmigration have to do with the actual method of reincarnation, that is, with the explanation of the actual physical processes which have to be undergone by the Ego in passing from the unembodied to the embodied state, and also with the roads, ways, or means of descent from the invisible to the visible plane. This has not yet been plainly explained in Theosophical books, because on the one hand it is a delicate matter, and on the other the details would not as yet be received even by Theosophists with credence, although one day they will be. And as these details are not of the greatest importance they are not now expounded. But as we know that no human body is formed without the union of the sexes, and that the germs for such production are locked up in the sexes and must come from food which is taken into the body, it is obvious that foods have something to do with the reincarnating of the Ego. Now if the road to reincarnation leads through certain food and none other, it may be possible that if the Ego gets entangled in food which will not lead to the germ of physical reproduction, a punishment is indicated where Manu says that such and such practices will lead to transmigration, which is then a "hindrance." I throw this out so far for the benefit of certain theosophists who read these and whose theories on this subject are now rather vague and in some instances based on quite other hypotheses.

The second explanation is, that inasmuch as nature intends us to use the matter which comes into our body and astral body for the purpose, among others, of benefitting the matter by the impress it gets from association with the human Ego, if we use it so as to give it only a brutal impression it must fly back to the animal kingdom to be absorbed there instead of being refined and kept on the human plane. And as all the matter which the human Ego gathered to it retains the stamp or photographic impression of the human being, the matter transmigrates to the lower level when given an animal impress by the Ego. This actual fact in the great chemical laboratory of nature could easily be misconstrued by the ignorant. But the present-day students know that once *Manas* the Thinker has arrived on the scene he does not return to baser forms; first, because he does not wish to, and second, because he cannot. For just as the blood in the body is prevented by valves from rushing back and engorging the heart, so in this greater system of universal circulation the door is shut behind the Thinker and prevents his retrocession. Reincarnation as a doctrine applying to the real man does not teach transmigration into kingdoms of nature below the human.

CHAPTER VIII

CHAPTER IX
Reincarnation Continued

IN the West, where the object of life is commercial, financial, social, or scientific success, that is, personal profit, aggrandizement, and power, the real life of man receives but little attention, and we, unlike the Orientals, give scant prominence to the doctrine of preexistence and reincarnation. That the church denies it is enough for many, with whom no argument is of any use. Relying on the church, they do not wish to disturb the serenity of their faith in dogmas that may be illogical; and as they have been taught that the church can bind them in hell, a blind fear of the anathema hurled at reincarnation in the Constantinople council about 500 A.D. would alone debar them from accepting the accursed theory. And the church in arguing on the doctrine urges the objection that if men are convinced that they will live many lives, the temptation to accept the present and do evil without check will be too strong. Absurd as this seems, it is put forward by learned Jesuits, who say men will rather have the present chance than wait for others. If there were no retribution at all this would be a good objection, but as Nature has also a Nemesis for every evil doer, and as each, under the law of Karma — which is that of cause and effect and perfect justice — must receive the exact consequences himself in every life for what good or bad deeds and thoughts he did and had in other lives, the basis for moral conduct is secure. It is safe under this system, since no man can by any possibility, or favor, or edict, or belief escape the consequences, and each one who grasps this doctrine will be moved by conscience and the whole power of nature to do well in order that he may receive good and become happy.

It is maintained that the idea of rebirth is uncongenial and unpleasant because on the one hand it is cold, allowing no sentiment to interfere, prohibiting us from renouncing at will a life which we have found to be sorrowful; and on the other, that there appears to be no chance under it for us to see our loved ones who have passed away before us. But whether we like it or not Nature's laws go forward unerringly, and sentiment or feeling can in no way avert the consequence that must follow a cause. If we eat bad food bad results must come. The glutton would have Nature permit him to gorge himself without the indigestion which will come, but Nature's laws are not to be thus put aside. Now, the objection to reincarnation that we will not see our loved ones in heaven as promised in dogmatic religion, presupposes a complete stoppage of the evolution and development of those who leave earth before ourselves, and also assumes that recognition is dependent on physical appearance. But as we progress in this life, so also must we progress upon leaving it, and it would be unfair to compel the others to await our arrival in order that we may recognize them. And if one reflects on the natural consequences of arising to heaven where all trammels are cast off, it must be apparent that those who have been there, say, twenty of mortal years before us must, in the nature of things mental and spiritual, have made a progress equal to many hundreds of years here under varied and very favorable circumstances. How then could we, arriving later and still imperfect, be able to recognize those who had been perfecting themselves in heaven with such advantages? And as we know that the body is left behind to disintegrate, so, it is evident, recognition cannot depend, in the spiritual and mental life, on physical appearance. For not only is this thus plain, but since we are aware that an unhandsome or deformed body often enshrines a glorious mind and pure soul, and that a beautifully formed exterior — such as in the case of the Borgias — may hide an incarnate devil in character, the physical form gives no guarantee of recognition in that world where the body is absent. And the mother who has lost a child who had grown to maturity must know that she loved the child when a baby as much as afterwards when the great alteration to later life had completely swept away the form and features of early youth. The Theosophists see that this objection can have no existence in the face of the eternal and pure life of the soul. And Theosophy also teaches that those who are like unto each other and love each other will be reincarnated together whenever the conditions permit. Whenever one of us has gone farther on the road to perfection, he will always be moved to help and comfort those who belong to the same family. But when one has become gross and selfish and wicked, no one would want his companionship in any life. Recognition depends on the inner sight and not on outward appearance; hence there is no force in this objection. And the other phase of it relating to loss of parent, child, or relative is based on the erroneous notion that as the parents give the child its body so also is given its soul. But soul is immortal and parentless; hence this objection is without a root.

CHAPTER IX

Some urge that Heredity invalidates Reincarnation. We urge it as proof. Heredity in giving us a body in any family provides the appropriate environment for the Ego. The Ego only goes into the family which either completely answers to its whole nature, or which gives an opportunity for the working out of its evolution, and which is also connected with it by reason of past incarnations or causes mutually set up. Thus the evil child may come to the presently good family because parents and child are indissolubly connected by past actions. It is a chance for redemption to the child and the occasion of punishment to the parents. This points to bodily heredity as a natural rule governing the bodies we must inhabit, just as the houses in a city will show the mind of the builders. And as we as well as our parents were the makers and influencers of bodies, took part in and are responsible for states of society in which the development of physical body and brain was either retarded or helped on, debased or the contrary, so we are in this life responsible for the civilization in which we now appear. But when we look at the characters in human bodies, great inherent differences are seen. This is due to the soul inside, who is suffering or enjoying in the family, nation, and race his own thoughts and acts in the past lives have made it inevitable he should incarnate with.

Heredity provides the tenement and also imposes those limitations of capacity of brain or body which are often a punishment and sometimes a help, but it does not affect the real Ego. The transmission of traits is a physical matter, and nothing more than the coming out into a nation of the consequences of the prior lives of all Egos who are to be in that race. The limitations imposed on the Ego by any family heredity are exact consequences of that Ego's prior lives. The fact that such physical traits and mental peculiarities are transmitted does not confute reincarnation, since we know that the guiding mind and real character of each are not the result of a body and brain but are peculiar to the Ego in its essential life. Transmission of trait and tendency by means of parent and body is exactly the mode selected by nature for providing the incarnating Ego with the proper tenement in which to carry on its work. Another mode would be impossible and subversive of order.

Again, those who dwell on the objection from heredity forget that they are accentuating similarities and overlooking divergencies. For while investigations on the line of heredity have recorded many transmitted traits, they have not done so in respect to divergencies from heredity vastly greater in number. Every mother knows that the children of a family are as different in character as the fingers on one hand — they are all from the same parents, but all vary in character and capacity.

But heredity as the great rule and as a complete explanation is absolutely overthrown by history, which shows no constant transmission of learning, power, and capacity. For instance, in the case of the ancient Egyptians long gone and their line of transmission shattered, we have no transmission to their descendants. If physical heredity settles the question of character, how has the great Egyptian character been lost? The same question holds in respect to other ancient and extinct nations. And taking an individual illustration we have the great musician Bach, whose direct descendants showed a decrease in musical ability leading to its final disappearance from the family stock. But Theosophy teaches that in both of these instances — as in all like them — the real capacity and ability have only disappeared from a family and national body, but are retained in the Egos who once exhibited them, being now incarnated in some other nation and family of the present time.

Suffering comes to nearly all men, and a great many live lives of sorrow from the cradle to the grave, so it is objected that reincarnation is unjust because we suffer for the wrong done by some other person in another life. This objection is based on the false notion that the person in the other life was some one else. But in every life it is the same person. When we come again we do not take up the body of some one else, nor another's deeds, but are like an actor who plays many parts, the same actor inside though the costumes and the lines recited differ in each new play. Shakespeare was right in saying that life is a play, for the great life of the soul is a drama, and each new life and rebirth another act in which we assume another part and put on a new dress, but all through it we are the self-same person. So instead of its being unjust, it is perfect justice, and in no other manner could justice be preserved.

But, it is said, if we reincarnate how is it that we do not remember the other life; and further, as we cannot remember the deeds for which we suffer is it not unjust for that reason? Those who ask this always ignore the fact that they also have enjoyment and reward in life and are content to accept them without question. For if it is unjust to be punished for deeds we do not remember, then it is also inequitable to be rewarded for other acts which have been forgotten. Mere entry into life is no fit foundation for any reward or punishment. Reward and punishment must be the just desert for prior conduct. Nature's law of justice is not imperfect, and it is only the imperfection of human justice that requires the offender to know and remember in this life a deed to which a penalty is annexed. In the prior life the doer was then quite aware of what he did, and nature affixes consequences to his acts, being thus just. We well know that she will make the effect follow the cause whatever we wish and whether we remember or forget what we did. If a baby is hurt in its first years by the nurse so as to lay the ground for a crippling disease in after life, as is often the case, the crippling disease will come although the child neither brought on the present cause nor remembered aught about it. But reincarnation, with its companion doctrine of Karma, rightly understood, shows how perfectly just the whole scheme of nature is.

Memory of a prior life is not needed to prove that we passed through that existence, nor is the fact of not remembering a good objection. We forget the greater part of the occurrences of the years and days of this life, but no one would say for that reason we did not go through these years. They were lived, and we retain but little of the details in the brain, but the entire effect of them on the character is kept and made a part of ourselves. The whole mass of detail of a life is preserved in the inner man to be one day fully brought back to the conscious memory in some other life when we are perfected. And even now, imperfect as we are and little as we know, the experiments in hypnotism show that all the smallest details are registered in what is for the present known as the sub-conscious mind. The theosophical doctrine is that not a single one of these happenings is forgotten in fact, and at the end of life when the eyes are closed and those about say we are dead every thought and circumstance of life flash vividly into and across the mind.

Many persons do, however, remember that they have lived before. Poets have sung of this, children know it well, until the constant living in an atmosphere of unbelief drives the recollection from their minds for the present, but all are subject to the limitations imposed upon the Ego by the new brain in each life. This is why we are not able to keep the pictures of the past, whether of this life or the preceding ones. The brain is the instrument for the memory of the soul, and, being new in each life with but a certain capacity, the Ego is only able to use it for the new life up to its capacity. That capacity will be fully availed of or the contrary, just according to the Ego's own desire and prior conduct, because such past living will have increased or diminished its power to overcome the forces of material existence.

By living according to the dictates of the soul the brain may at least be made porous to the soul's recollections; if the contrary sort of a life is led, then more and more will clouds obscure that reminiscence. But as the brain had no part in the life last lived, it is in general unable to remember. And this is a wise law, for we should be very miserable if the deeds and scenes of our former lives were not hidden from our view until by discipline we become able to bear a knowledge of them.

Another objection brought up is that under the doctrine of reincarnation it is not possible to account for the increase of the world's population. This assumes that we know surely that its population has increased and are keeping informed of its fluctuations. But it is not certain that the inhabitants of the globe have increased, and, further, vast numbers of people are annually destroyed of whom we know nothing. In China year after year many thousands have been carried off by flood. Statistics of famine have not been made. We do not know by how many thousands the deaths in Africa exceed the births in any year. The objection is based on imperfect tables which only have to do with western lands. It also assumes that there are fewer Egos out of incarnation and waiting to come in than the number of those inhabiting bodies, and this is incorrect. Annie Besant has put this well in her "Reincarnation" by saying that the inhabited globe resembles a hall in a town which is filled from the much greater population of the town outside; the number in the hall may vary, but there is a constant source of supply from the town. It is true that so far as concerns this globe the number of Egos belonging to it is definite; but no one knows what that quantity is nor what is the total capacity of the earth for sustaining them. The statisticians of the day are chiefly in the West, and their tables embrace but a small section of the history of man. They cannot say how many persons were incarnated on the earth at any prior date when the globe was full in all parts, hence the quantity of egos willing or waiting to be reborn is unknown to the men of today. The Masters of theosophical knowledge say that the total number of such egos is vast, and for that reason the supply of those for the occupation of bodies to be born over and above the number that die is sufficient. Then too it must be borne in mind that each ego for itself varies the length of stay in the *post-mortem* states. They do not reincarnate at the same interval, but come out of the state after death at different rates, and whenever there occurs a great number of deaths by war, pestilence, or famine, there is at once a rush of souls to incarnation, either in the same place or in some other place or race. The earth is so small a globe in the vast assemblage of inhabitable planets there is a sufficient supply of Egos for incarnation here. But with due respect to those who put this objection, I do not see that it has the slightest force or any relation to the truth of the doctrine of reincarnation.

CHAPTER X

Arguments Supporting Reincarnation

UNLESS we deny the immortality of man and the existence of soul, there are no sound arguments against the doctrine of preexistence and re-birth save such as rest on the dictum of the church that each soul is a new creation. This dictum can be supported only by blind dogmatism, for given a soul we must sooner or later arrive at the theory of rebirth, because even if each soul is new on this earth it must keep on living somewhere after passing away, and in view of the known order of nature will have other bodies in other planets or spheres. Theosophy applies to the self — the thinker — the same laws which are seen everywhere in operation throughout nature, and those are all varieties of the great law that effects follow causes and no effect is without a cause. The soul's immortality — believed in by the mass of humanity — demands embodiment here or elsewhere, and to be embodied means reincarnation. If we come to this earth for but a few years and then go to some other, the soul must be embodied there as well as here, and if we have travelled from some other world we must have had there too our proper vesture. The powers of mind and the laws governing its motion, its attachment, and its detachment as given in theosophical philosophy show that its reembodiment must be here, where it moved and worked, until such time as the mind is able to overcome the forces which chain it to this globe. To permit the involved entity to transfer itself to another scene of action before it had overcome all the causes drawing it here and without its having worked out its responsibilities to other entities in the same stream of evolution would be unjust and contrary to the powerful occult laws and forces which continually operate upon it. The early Christian Fathers saw this, and taught that the soul had fallen into matter and was obliged by the law of its nature to toil upward again to the place from which it came. They used an old Greek hymn which ran:

Eternal Mind, thy seedling spark,
Through this thin vase of clay,
Athwart the waves of chaos dark
Emits a timorous ray.
This mind enfolding soul is sown,
Incarnate germ in earth:
In pity, blessed Lord, then own
What claims in Thee its birth.
Far forth from Thee, thou central fire,
To earth's sad bondage cast,
Let not the trembling spark expire;
Absorb thine own at last!

Each human being has a definite character different from every other human being, and masses of beings aggregated into nations show as wholes that the national force and distinguishing peculiarities go to make up a definite and separate national character. These differences, both individual and national, are due to essential character and not to education. Even the doctrine of the survival of the fittest should show this, for the fitness cannot come from nothing but must at last show itself from the coming to the surface of the actual inner character. And as both individuals and nations among those who are ahead in the struggle with nature exhibit an immense force in their character, we must find a place and time where the force was evolved. These, Theosophy says, are this earth and the whole period during which the human race has been on the planet.

So, then, while heredity has something to do with the difference in character as to force and morale, swaying the soul and mind a little and furnishing also the appropriate place for receiving reward and punishment, it is not the cause for the essential nature shown by every one.

But all these differences, such as those shown by babes from birth, by adults as character comes forth more and more, and by nations in their history, are due to long experience gained during many lives on earth, are the outcome of the soul's own evolution. A survey of one short human life gives no ground for the production of his inner nature. It is needful that each soul should have all possible experience, and one life cannot give this even under the best conditions. It would be folly for the Almighty to put us here for such a short time, only to remove us just when we had begun to see the object of life and the possibilities in it. The mere selfish desire of a person to escape the trials and discipline of life is not enough to set nature's laws aside, so the soul must be reborn until it has ceased to set in motion the cause of rebirth, after having developed character up to its possible limit as indicated by all the varieties of human nature, when every experience has been passed through, and not until all of truth that can be known has been acquired. The vast disparity among men in respect to capacity compels us, if we wish to ascribe justice to Nature or to God, to admit reincarnation and to trace the origin of the disparity back to the past lives of the Ego. For people are as much hindered and handicapped, abused and made the victims of seeming injustice because of limited capacity, as they are by reason of circumstances of birth or education. We see the uneducated rising above circumstances of family and training, and often those born in good families have very small capacity; but the troubles of nations and families arise from want of capacity more than from any other cause. And if we consider savage races only, there the seeming injustice is enormous. For many savages have good actual brain capacity but still are savage. This is because the Ego in that body is still savage and undeveloped, for in contrast to the savage there are many civilized men with small actual brain force who are not savage in nature because the indwelling Ego has had long experience in civilization during other lives, and being a more developed soul has power to use the brain instrument to its highest limit.

Each man feels and knows that he has an individuality of his own, a personal identity which bridges over not only the gaps made by sleep but also those sometimes supervening on temporary lesions in the brain. This identity never breaks from beginning to end of life in the normal person, and only the persistence and eternal character of the soul will account for it.

So, ever since we began to remember, we know that our personal identity has not failed us, no matter how bad may be our memory. This disposes of the argument that identity depends on recollection, for the reason that if it did depend alone on recollection we should each day have to begin over again, as we cannot remember the events of the past in detail, and some minds remember but little yet feel their personal identity. And as it is often seen that some who remember the least insist as strongly as the others on their personal identity, that persistence of feeling must come from the old and immortal soul.

Viewing life and its probable object, with all the varied experience possible for man, one must be forced to the conclusion that a single life is not enough for carrying out all that is intended by Nature, to say nothing of what man himself desires to do. The scale of variety in experience is enormous. There is a vast range of powers latent in man which we see may be developed if opportunity be given. Knowledge infinite in scope and diversity lies before us, and especially in these days when special investigation is the rule. We perceive that we have high aspirations with no time to reach up to their measure, while the great troop of passions and desires, selfish motives and ambitions, war with us and among themselves, pursuing us even to the door of death. All these have to be tried, conquered, used, subdued. One life is not enough for all this. To say that we have but one life here with such possibilities put before us and impossible of development is to make the universe and life a huge and cruel joke perpetrated by a powerful God who is thus accused, by those who believe in a special creation of souls, of triumphing and playing with puny man just because that man is small and the creature of the Almighty. A human life at most is seventy years; statistics reduce this to about forty; and out of that little remainder a large part is spent in sleep and another part in childhood. Thus in one life it is perfectly impossible to attain to the merest fraction of what Nature evidently has in view. We see many truths vaguely which a life gives us no time to grasp, and especially is this so when men have to make such a struggle to live at all. Our faculties are small or dwarfed or weak; one life gives no opportunity to alter this; we perceive other powers latent in us that cannot possibly be brought out in such a small space of time; and we have much more than a suspicion that the extent of the field of truth is vastly greater than the narrow circle we are confined to. It is not reasonable to suppose that either God or nature projects us into a body simply to fill us with bitterness because we can have no other opportunity here, but rather we must conclude that a series of incarnations has led to the present condition, and that the process of coming here again and again must go on for the purpose of affording us the opportunity needed.

The mere fact of dying is not of itself enough to bring about development of faculties or the elimination of wrong tendency and inclination. If we assume that upon entering heaven we at once acquire all knowledge and purity, then that state after death is reduced to a dead level and life itself with all its discipline is shorn of every meaning. Some of the churches teach of a school of discipline after death where it is impudently stated that the Apostles themselves, well known to be ignorant men, are to be the teachers. This is absurd and devoid of any basis or reason in the natural order. Besides, if there is to be such subsequent discipline, why were we projected into life at all? And why after the suffering and the error committed are we taken from the place where we did our acts? The only solution left is in reincarnation. We come back to earth because on it and with the beings upon it our deeds were performed; because it is the only proper place where punishment and reward can be justly meted out; because here is the only natural spot in which to continue the struggle toward perfection, toward the development of the faculties we have and the destruction of the wickedness in us. Justice to ourselves and to all other beings demands it, for we cannot live for ourselves, and it would be unjust to permit some of us to escape, leaving those who were participants with us to remain or to be plunged into a hell of eternal duration.

The persistence of savagery, the rise and decay of nations and civilizations, the total extinction of nations, all demand an explanation found nowhere but in reincarnation. Savagery remains because there are still Egos whose experience is so limited that they are still savage; they will come up into higher races when ready. Races die out because the Egos have had enough of the experience that sort of race gives. So we find the red Indian, the Hottentot, the Easter Islanders, and others as examples of races deserted by high Egos and as they are dying away other souls who have had no higher life in the past enter into the bodies of the race to go on using them for the purpose of gaining such experience as the race body will give. A race could not possibly arise and then suddenly go out. We see that such is not the case, but science has no explanation; it simply says that this is the fact, that nations decay. But in this explanation no account is taken of the inner man nor of the recondite subtle and occult laws that unite to make a race. Theosophy shows that the energy drawn together has to expend itself gradually, and therefore the reproduction of bodies of the character of that race will go on, though the Egos are not compelled to inhabit bodies of that sort any longer than while they are of the same development as the race. Hence a time comes when the whole mass of Egos which built up the race leaves it for another physical environment more like themselves. The economy of Nature will not permit the physical race to suddenly fade away, and so in the real order of evolution other and less progressed Egos come in and use the forms provided, keeping up the production of new bodies but less and less in number each century. These lower Egos are not able to keep up to the limit of the capacity of the congeries of energies left by the other Egos, and so while the new set gains as much experience as is possible the race in time dies out after passing through its decay. This is the explanation of what we may call descending savagery, and no other theory will meet the facts. It has been sometimes thought by ethnologists that the more civilized races kill off the other, but the fact is that in consequence of the great difference between the Egos inhabiting the old race body and the energy of that body itself, the females begin to be sterile, and thus slowly but surely the number of deaths exceeds the births. China itself is in process of decay, she being now in the almost stationary stage just before the rush downward. Great civilizations like those of Egypt and Babylon have gone because the souls who made them have long ago reincarnated in the great conquering nations of Europe and the present American continents. As nations and races they have been totally reincarnated and born again for greater and higher purposes than ever. Of all the old races the Aryan Indian alone yet remains as the preserver of the old doctrines. It will one day rise again to its old heights of glory.

CHAPTER X

The appearance of geniuses and great minds in families destitute of these qualities, as well as the extinction from a family of the genius shown by some ancestor, can only be met by the law of rebirth. Napoleon the First came in a family wholly unlike him in power and force. Nothing in his heredity will explain his character. He said himself, as told in the Memoirs of Prince Talleyrand, that he was Charlemagne. Only by assuming for him a long series of lives giving the right line of evolution or cause for his mind and nature and force to be brought out, can we have the slightest idea why he or any other great genius appeared at all. Mozart when an infant could compose orchestral scores. This was not due to heredity, for such a score is not natural, but is forced, mechanical, and wholly conventional, yet he understood it without schooling. How? Because he was a musician reincarnated, with a musical brain furnished by his family and thus not impeded in his endeavors to show forth his musical knowledge. But stronger yet is the case of Blind Tom, a negro whose family could not by any possibility have a knowledge of the piano, a modern instrument, so as to transmit that knowledge to the atoms of his body, yet he had great musical power and knew the present mechanical musical scale on the piano. There are hundreds of examples like these among the many prodigies who have appeared to the world's astonishment. In India there are many histories of sages born with complete knowledge of philosophy and the like, and doubtless in all nations the same can be met with. This bringing back of knowledge also explains instinct, for that is no more than recollection divisible into physical and mental memory. It is seen in the child and the animal, and is no more than the result of previous experience. And whether we look at the new-born babe flinging out its arms for self-protection, or the animal with very strong instinctual power, or the bee building a cell on the rules of geometry, it is all the effect of reincarnation acting either in the mind or physical cell, for under what was first laid down no atom is devoid of life, consciousness, and intelligence of its own.

In the case of the musician Bach we have proof that heredity counts for nothing if the Ego is not advanced, for his genius was not borne down his family line; it gradually faded out, finally leaving the family stream entirely. So, too, the coming of idiots or vicious children to parents who are good, pure, or highly intellectual is explained in the same way. They are cases where heredity is set at nought by a wholly bad or deficient Ego.

And lastly, the fact that certain inherent ideas are common to the whole race is explained by the sages as due to recollection of such ideas, which were implanted in the human mind at the very beginning of its evolutionary career on this planet by those brothers and sages who learned their lessons and were perfected in former ages long before the development of this globe began. No explanation for inherent ideas is offered by science that will do more than say, "they exist." These were actually taught to the mass of Egos who are engaged in this earth's evolution; they were imprinted or burned into their natures, and always recollected; they follow the Ego through the long pilgrimage.

It has been often thought that the opposition to reincarnation has been solely based on prejudice, when not due to a dogma which can only stand when the mind is bound down and prevented from using its own powers. It is a doctrine the most noble of all, and with its companion one of Karma, next to be considered, it alone gives the basis for ethics. There is no doubt in my mind that the founder of Christianity took it for granted and that its present absence from that religion is the reason for the contradiction between the professed ethics of Christian nations and their actual practises which are so contrary to the morals given out by Jesus.

CHAPTER X

CHAPTER XI
Karma

KARMA is an unfamiliar word for Western ears. It is the name adopted by Theosophists of the nineteenth century for one of the most important of the laws of nature. Ceaseless in its operation, it bears alike upon planets, systems of planets, races, nations, families, and individuals. It is the twin doctrine to reincarnation. So inextricably interlaced are these two laws that it is almost impossible to properly consider one apart from the other. No spot or being in the universe is exempt from the operation of Karma, but all are under its sway, punished for error by it yet beneficently led on, through discipline, rest, and reward, to the distant heights of perfection. It is a law so comprehensive in its sweep, embracing at once our physical and our moral being, that it is only by paraphrase and copious explanation one can convey its meaning in English. For that reason the Sanskrit term *Karma* was adopted to designate it.

Applied to man's moral life it is the law of ethical causation, justice, reward and punishment; the cause for birth and rebirth, yet equally the means for escape from incarnation. Viewed from another point it is merely effect flowing from cause, action and reaction, exact result for every thought and act. It is act and the result of act; for the word's literal meaning is action. Theosophy views the Universe as an intelligent whole, hence every motion in the Universe is an action of that whole leading to results, which themselves become causes for further results. Viewing it thus broadly, the ancient Hindus said that every being up to Brahma was under the rule of Karma.

It is not a being but a law, the universal law of harmony which unerringly restores all disturbance to equilibrium. In this the theory conflicts with the ordinary conception about God, built up from the Jewish system, which assumes that the Almighty as a thinking entity, extraneous to the Cosmos, builds up, finds his construction inharmonious, out of proportion, errant, and disturbed, and then has to pull down, destroy, or punish that which he created. This has either caused thousands to live in fear of God, in compliance with his assumed commands, with the selfish object of obtaining reward and securing escape from his wrath, or has plunged them into darkness which comes from a denial of all spiritual life. But as there is plainly, indeed painfully, evident to every human being a constant destruction going on in and around us, a continual war not only among men but everywhere through the whole solar system, causing sorrow in all directions, reason requires a solution of the riddle. The poor, who see no refuge or hope, cry aloud to a God who makes no reply, and then envy springs up in them when they consider the comforts and opportunities of the rich. They see the rich profligates, the wealthy fools, enjoying themselves unpunished. Turning to the teacher of religion, they meet the reply to their questioning of the justice which will permit such misery to those who did nothing requiring them to be born with no means, no opportunities for education, no capacity to overcome social, racial, or circumstantial obstacles, "It is the will of God." Parents produce beloved offspring who are cut off by death at an untimely hour, just when all promised well. They too have no answer to the question "Why am I thus afflicted?" but the same unreasonable reference to an inaccessible God whose arbitrary will causes their misery. Thus in every walk of life, loss, injury, persecution, deprivation of opportunity, nature's own forces working to destroy the happiness of man, death, reverses, disappointment continually beset good and evil men alike. But nowhere is there any answer or relief save in the ancient truths that each man is the maker and fashioner of his own destiny, the only one who sets in motion the causes for his own happiness and misery. In one life he sows and in the next he reaps. Thus on and forever, the law of Karma leads him.

Karma is a beneficent law wholly merciful, relentlessly just, for true mercy is not favor but impartial justice.

> "My brothers! each man's life
> The outcome of his former living is;
> The bygone wrongs bring forth sorrows and woes,
> The bygone right breeds bliss. . . .
> This is the doctrine of Karma."

How is the present life affected by that bygone right and wrong act, and is it always by way of punishment? Is Karma only fate under another name, an already fixed and formulated destiny from which no escape is possible, and which therefore might make us careless of act or thought that cannot affect destiny? It is not fatalism. Everything done in a former body has consequences which in the new birth the Ego must enjoy or suffer, for, as St. Paul said: "Brethren, be not deceived, God is not mocked, for whatsoever a man soweth that shall he also reap." For the effect is in the cause, and Karma produces the manifestation of it in the body, brain, and mind furnished by reincarnation. And as a cause set up by one man has a distinct relation to him as a center from which it came, so each one experiences the results of his own acts. We may sometimes seem to receive effects solely from the acts of others, but this is the result of our own acts and thoughts in this or some prior life. We perform our acts in company with others always, and the acts with their underlying thoughts have relation always to other persons and to ourselves.

No act is performed without a thought at its root either at the time of performance or as leading to it. These thoughts are lodged in that part of man which we have called *Manas* — the mind, and there remain as subtle but powerful links with magnetic threads that enmesh the solar system, and through which various effects are brought out. The theory put forward in earlier pages that the whole system to which this globe belongs is alive, conscious on every plane, though only in man showing self-consciousness, comes into play here to explain how the thought under the act in this life may cause result in this or the next birth. The marvellous modern experiments in hypnotism show that the slightest impression, no matter how far back in the history of the person, may be waked up to life, thus proving it is not lost but only latent. Take for instance the case of a child born humpbacked and very short, the head sunk between the shoulders, the arms long and legs curtailed. Why is this? His karma for thoughts and acts in a prior life. He reviled, persecuted, or otherwise injured a deformed person so persistently or violently as to imprint in his own immortal mind the deformed picture of his victim. For in proportion to the intensity of his thought will be the intensity and depth of the picture. It is exactly similar to the exposure of the sensitive photographic plate, whereby, just as the exposure is long or short, the impression in the plate is weak or deep. So this thinker and actor — the Ego — coming again to rebirth carries with him this picture, and if the family to which he is attracted for birth has similar physical tendencies in its stream, the mental picture causes the newly-forming astral body to assume a deformed shape by electrical and magnetic osmosis through the mother of the child. And as all beings on earth are indissolubly joined together, the misshapen child is the karma of the parents also an exact consequence for similar acts and thoughts on their part in other lives. Here is an exactitude of justice which no other theory will furnish.

But as we often see a deformed human being — continuing the instance merely for the purpose of illustration — having a happy disposition, an excellent intellect, sound judgment, and every good moral quality, this very instance leads us to the conclusion that karma must be of several different kinds in every individual case, and also evidently operates in more than one department of our being, with the possibility of being pleasant in effect for one portion of our nature and unpleasant for another.

Karma is of three sorts:

First — that which has not begun to produce any effect in our lives owing to the operation on us of some other karmic causes. This is under a law well known to physicists, that two opposing forces tend to neutrality, and that one force may be strong enough to temporarily prevent the operation of another one. This law works on the unseen mental and karmic planes or spheres of being just as it does on the material ones. The force of a certain set of bodily, mental, and psychical faculties with their tendencies may wholly inhibit the operation on us of causes with which we are connected, because the whole nature of each person is used in the carrying out of this law. Hence the weak and mediocre furnish a weak focus for karma, and in them the general result of a lifetime is limited, although they may feel it all to be very heavy. But that person who has a wide and deep-reaching character and much force will feel the operation of a greater quantity of karma than the weaker person.

Second — that karma which we are now making or storing up by our thoughts and acts, and which will operate in the future when the appropriate body, mind, and environment are taken up by the incarnating Ego in some other life, or whenever obstructive karma is removed.

This bears both on the present life and the next one. For one may in this life come to a point where, all previous causes being worked out, new karma, or that which is unexpended, must begin to operate.

Under this are those cases where men have sudden reverses of fortune or changes for the better either in circumstances or character. A very important bearing of this is on our present conduct. While old karma must work out and cannot be stopped, it is wise for the man to so think and act now under present circumstances, no matter what they are, that he shall produce no bad or prejudicial causes for the next rebirth or for later years in this life. Rebellion is useless, for the law works on whether we weep or rejoice.

CHAPTER XI

The great French engineer, de Lesseps, is a good example of this class of karma. Raised to a high pitch of glory and achievement for many years of his life, he suddenly falls covered with shame through the Panama canal scandal. Whether he was innocent or guilty, he has the shame of the connection of his name with a national enterprise all besmirched with bribery and corruption that involved high officials. This was the operation of old karmic causes on him the very moment those which had governed his previous years were exhausted. Napoleon I is another, for he rose to a very great fame, then suddenly fell and died in exile and disgrace. Many other cases will occur to every thoughtful reader.

Third — that karma which has begun to produce results. It is the operating now in this life on us of causes set up in previous lives in company with other Egos. And it is in operation because, being most adapted to the family stock, the individual body, astral body, and race tendencies of the present incarnation, it exhibits itself plainly, while other unexpended karma awaits its regular turn.

These three classes of karma govern men, animals, worlds, and periods of evolution. Every effect flows from a cause precedent, and as all beings are constantly being reborn they are continually experiencing the effects of their thoughts and acts (which are themselves causes) of a prior incarnation. And thus each one answers, as St. Matthew says, for every word and thought; none can escape either by prayer, or favor, or force, or any other intermediary.

Now as karmic causes are divisible into three classes, they must have various fields in which to work. They operate upon man in his mental and intellectual nature, in his psychical or soul nature, and in his body and circumstances. The spiritual nature of man is never affected or operated upon by karma.

One species of karma may act on the three specified planes of our nature at the same time to the same degree, or there may be a mixture of the causes, some on one plane and some on another. Take a deformed person who has a fine mind and a deficiency in his soul nature. Here punitive or unpleasant karma is operating on his body while in his mental and intellectual nature good karma is being experienced, but psychically the karma, or cause, being of an indifferent sort the result is indifferent. In another person other combinations appear. He has a fine body and favorable circumstances, but the character is morose, peevish, irritable, revengeful, morbid, and disagreeable to himself and others. Here good physical karma is at work with very bad mental, intellectual, and psychical karma. Cases will occur to readers of persons born in high station having every opportunity and power, yet being imbecile or suddenly becoming insane.

And just as all these phases of the law of karma have sway over the individual man, so they similarly operate upon races, nations, and families. Each race has its karma as a whole. If it be good that race goes forward. If bad it goes out — annihilated as a race — though the souls concerned take up their karma in other races and bodies. Nations cannot escape their national karma, and any nation that has acted in a wicked manner must suffer some day, be it soon or late. The karma of the nineteenth century in the West is the karma of Israel, for even the merest tyro can see that the Mosaic influence is the strongest in the

European and American nations. The old Aztec and other ancient American peoples died out because their own karma — the result of their own life as nations in the far past — fell upon and destroyed them. With nations this heavy operation of karma is always through famine, war, convulsion of nature, and the sterility of the women of the nation. The latter cause comes near the end and sweeps the whole remnant away. And the individual in race or nation is warned by this great doctrine that if he falls into indifference of thought and act, thus molding himself into the general average karma of his race or nation, that national and race karma will at last carry him off in the general destiny. This is why teachers of old cried, "Come ye out and be ye separate."

With reincarnation the doctrine of karma explains the misery and suffering of the world, and no room is left to accuse Nature of injustice.

The misery of any nation or race is the direct result of the thoughts and acts of the Egos who make up the race or nation. In the dim past they did wickedly and now suffer. They violated the laws of harmony. The immutable rule is that harmony must be restored if violated. So these Egos suffer in making compensation and establishing the equilibrium of the occult cosmos. The whole mass of Egos must go on incarnating and reincarnating in the nation or race until they have all worked out to the end the causes set up. Though the nation may for a time disappear as a physical thing, the Egos that made it do not leave the world, but come out as the makers of some new nation in which they must go on with the task and take either punishment or reward as accords with their karma. Of this law the old Egyptians are an illustration. They certainly rose to a high point of development, and as certainly they were extinguished as a nation. But the souls — the old Egos — live on and are now fulfilling their self-made destiny as some other nation now in our period. They may be the new American nation, or the Jews fated to wander up and down in the world and suffer much at the hands of others. This process is perfectly just. Take, for instance, the United States and the Red Indians. The latter have been most shamefully treated by the nation. The Indian Egos will be reborn in the new and conquering people, and as members of that great family will be the means themselves of bringing on the due results for such acts as were done against them when they had red bodies. Thus it has happened before, and so it will come about again.

Individual unhappiness in any life is thus explained:

(*a*) It is punishment for evil done in past lives; or (*b*) it is discipline taken up by the Ego for the purpose of eliminating defects or acquiring fortitude and sympathy. When defects are eliminated it is like removing the obstruction in an irrigating canal which then lets the water flow on. Happiness is explained in the same way: the result of prior lives of goodness.

The scientific and self-compelling basis for right ethics is found in these and in no other doctrines. For if right ethics are to be practised merely for themselves, men will not see why, and have never been able to see why, for that reason they should do right. If ethics are to be followed from fear, man is degraded and will surely evade; if the favor of the Almighty, not based on law or justice, be the reason, then we will have just what prevails today — a code given by

Jesus to the west professed by nations and not practised save by the few who would in any case be virtuous.

On this subject the Adepts have written the following to be found in the *Secret Doctrine*:

Nor would the ways of Karma be inscrutable were men to work in union and harmony, instead of disunion and strife. For our ignorance of those ways — which one portion of mankind calls the ways of Providence, dark and intricate, while another sees in them the action of blind Fatalism, and a third, simple chance, with neither gods nor devils to guide them — would surely disappear, if we would but attribute all these to their correct cause. With right knowledge, or at any rate with a confident conviction that our neighbors will no more work to hurt us than we would think of harming them, the two-thirds of the World's evil would vanish into thin air. Were no man to hurt his brother, Karma-Nemesis would have neither cause to work for, nor weapons to act through. . . . We cut these numerous windings in our destinies daily with our own hands, while we imagine that we are pursuing a track on the royal high road of respectability and duty, and then complain of those ways being so intricate and so dark. We stand bewildered before the mystery of our own making, and the riddles of life that *we will not* solve, and then accuse the great Sphinx of devouring us. But verily there is not an accident in our lives, not a misshapen day, or a misfortune, that could not be traced back to our own doings in this or in another life. . . .

. . . Knowledge of Karma gives the conviction that if —

". . . . virtue in distress, and vice in triumph
Make atheists of mankind,"

it is only because that mankind has ever shut its eyes to the great truth that man is himself his own saviour as his own destroyer. That he need not accuse Heaven and the gods, Fates and Providence, of the apparent injustice that reigns in the midst of humanity. But let him rather remember and repeat this bit of Grecian wisdom, which warns man to forbear accusing *That* which —

> ". . . . ."
>
> "Just, though mysterious, leads us on unerring
> Through ways unmark'd from guilt to punishment . . ."

— which are now the ways and the high road on which move onward the great European nations. The Western Aryans had, every nation and tribe, like their Eastern brethren of the Fifth Race, their Golden and their Iron ages, their period of comparative irresponsibility, or the Satya age of purity, while now, several of them have reached their Iron Age, the *Kali Yuga,* an age BLACK WITH HORRORS. . . .

. . . This state will last . . . until we begin acting from *within* instead of ever following impulses from *without* . . . Until then the only palliative to the evils of life is union and harmony — a Brotherhood in ACTU, and *altruism* not simply in name.

CHAPTER XI

CHAPTER XII
Kama Loka

LET us now consider the states of man after the death of the body and before birth, having looked over the whole field of the evolution of things and beings in a general way. This brings up at once the questions: Is there any heaven or hell, and what are they? Are they states or places? Is there a spot in space where they may be found and to which we go or from where we come? We must also go back to the subject of the fourth principle of the constitution of man, that called *Kama* in Sanskrit and desire or passion in English. Bearing in mind what was said about that principle, and also the teaching in respect to the astral body and the Astral Light, it will be easier to understand what is taught about the two states *ante* and *post mortem.* In chronological order we go into *kama loka* — or the plane of desire — first on the demise of the body, and then the higher principles, the real man, fall into the state of *Devachan.* After dealing with *kama loka* it will be more easy to study the question of *Devachan.*

The breath leaves the body and we say the man is dead, but that is only the beginning of death; it proceeds on other planes. When the frame is cold and eyes closed, all the forces of the body and mind rush through the brain, and by a series of pictures the whole life just ended is imprinted indelibly on the inner man not only in a general outline but down to the smallest detail of even the most minute and fleeting impression. At this moment, though every indication leads the physician to pronounce for death and though to all intents and purposes the person is dead to this life, the real man is busy in the brain, and not until his work there is ended is the person gone. When this solemn work is over the astral body detaches itself from the physical, and, life energy having departed, the remaining five principles are in the plane of *kama loka.*

The natural separation of the principles brought about by death divides the total man into three parts:

First, the visible body with all its elements left to further disintegration on the earth plane, where all that it is composed of is in time resolved into the different physical departments of nature;

Second, the *kama rupa* made up of the astral body and the passions and desires, which also begins at once to go to pieces on the astral plane;

Third, the real man, the upper triad of *Atma-Buddhi-Manas,* deathless but now out of earth conditions, devoid of body, begins in *devachan* to function solely as mind clothed in a very ethereal vesture which it will shake off when the time comes for it to return to earth.

Kama loka — or the place of desire — is the astral region penetrating and surrounding the earth. As a place it is on and in and about the earth. Its extent is to a measurable distance from the earth, but the ordinary laws obtaining here do not obtain there, and entities therein are not under the same conditions as to space and time as we are. As a state it is metaphysical, though that metaphysic relates to the astral plane. It is called the plane of desire because it relates to the fourth principle, and in it the ruling force is desire devoid of and divorced from intelligence. It is an astral sphere intermediate between earthly and heavenly life. Beyond any doubt it is the origin of the Christian theory of purgatory, where the soul undergoes penance for evil done and from which it can be released by prayer and other ceremonies or offerings. The fact underlying this superstition is that the soul may be detained in *kama loka* by the enormous force of some unsatisfied desire, and cannot get rid of the astral and kamic clothing until that desire is satisfied by some one on earth or by the soul itself. But if the person was pure minded and of high aspirations, the separation of the principles on that plane is soon completed, permitting the higher triad to go into *Devachan.* Being the purely astral sphere, it partakes of the nature of the astral matter which is essentially earthly and devilish, and in it all the forces work undirected by soul or conscience. It is the slag-pit, as it were, of the great furnace of life, where nature provides for the sloughing off of elements which have no place in *Devachan,* and for that reason it must have many degrees, every one of which was noted by the ancients. These degrees are known in Sanskrit as *lokas* or places in a metaphysical sense. Human life is very varied as to character and other potentialities, and for each of these the appropriate place after death is provided, thus making *kama loka* an infinitely varied sphere. In life some of the differences among men are modified and some inhibited by a similarity of body and heredity, but in *kama loka* all the hidden desires and passions are let loose in consequence of the absence of body, and for that reason the state is vastly more diversified than the life plane. Not only is it necessary to provide for the natural varieties and differences, but also for those caused by the manner of death, about which something shall be said. And all these various divisions are but the natural result of the life thoughts and last thoughts of the persons who die on earth. It is beyond the scope of this work to go into a description of all these degrees, inasmuch as volumes would be needed to describe them, and then but few would understand.

To deal with *kama loka* compels us to deal also with the fourth principle in the classification of man's constitution, and arouses a conflict with modern ideas and education on the subject of the desires and passions. It is generally supposed that the desires and passions are inherent tendencies in the individual, and they have an altogether unreal and misty appearance for the ordinary student. But in this system of philosophy they are not merely inherent in the individual nor are they due to the body *per se.* While the man is living in the world the desires and passions — the principle *kama* — have no separate life apart from the astral and inner man, being, so to say, diffused throughout his being. But as they coalesce with the astral body after death and thus form an entity with its own term of life, though without soul, very important questions arise. During mortal life the desires and passions are guided by the mind and soul; after death they work without guidance from the former master; while we live we are responsible for them and their effects, and when we have left this life we are still responsible, although they go on working and making effects on others while they last as the sort of entity I have described, and without our direct guidance. In this is seen the continuance of responsibility. They are a portion of the *skandhas* — well known in eastern philosophy

— which are the aggregates that make up the man. The body includes one set of the *skandhas*, the astral man another, the *kama* principle is another set, and still others pertain to other parts. In *kama* are the really active and important ones which control rebirths and lead to all the varieties of life and circumstance upon each rebirth. They are being made from day to day under the law that every thought combines instantly with one of the elemental forces of nature, becoming to that extent an entity which will endure in accordance with the strength of the thought as it leaves the brain, and all of these are inseparably connected with the being who evolved them. There is no way of escaping; all we can do is to have thoughts of good quality, for the highest of the Masters themselves are not exempt from this law, but they "people their current in space" with entities powerful for good alone.

Now in *kama loka* this mass of desire and thought exists very definitely until the conclusion of its disintegration, and then the remainder consists of the essence of these *skandhas,* connected, of course, with the being that evolved and had them. They can no more be done away with than we can blot out the universe. Hence they are said to remain until the being comes out of *devachan,* and then at once by the law of attraction they are drawn to the being, who from them as germ or basis builds up a new set of *skandhas* for the new life. *Kama loka* therefore is distinguished from the earth plane by reason of the existence therein, uncontrolled and unguided, of the mass of passions and desires; but at the same time earth-life is also a *kama loka,* since it is largely governed by the principle *kama,* and will be so until at a far distant time in the course of evolution the races of men shall have developed the fifth and sixth principle, thus throwing *kama* into its own sphere and freeing earth-life from its influence.

The astral man in *kama loka* is a mere shell devoid of soul and mind, without conscience and also unable to act unless vivified by forces outside of itself. It has that which seems like an animal or automatic consciousness due wholly to the very recent association with the human Ego. For under the principle laid down in another chapter, every atom going to make up the man has a memory of its own which is capable of lasting a length of time in proportion to the force given it. In the case of a very material and gross or selfish person the force lasts longer than in any other, and hence in that case the automatic consciousness will be more definite and bewildering to one who without knowledge dabbles with necromancy. Its purely astral portion contains and carries the record of all that ever passed before the person when living, for one of the qualities of the astral substance is to absorb all scenes and pictures and the impressions of all thoughts, to keep them, and to throw them forth by reflection when the conditions permit. This astral shell, cast off by every man at death, would be a menace to all men were it not in every case, except one which shall be mentioned, devoid of all the higher principles which are the directors. But those guiding constituents being disjoined from the shell, it wavers and floats about from place to place without any will of its own, but governed wholly by attractions in the astral and magnetic fields.

It is possible for the real man — called the spirit by some — to communicate with us immediately after death for a few brief moments, but, those passed, the soul has no more to do with earth until reincarnated. What can and do influence the sensitive and the medium from out of this sphere are the shells I have described. Soulless and conscienceless, these in no sense are the spirits of our deceased ones. They are the clothing thrown off by the inner man, the brutal earthly portion discarded in the flight to *devachan,* and so have always been considered by the ancients as devils — our personal devils — because essentially astral, earthly, and passional. It would be strange indeed if this shell, after being for so long the vehicle of the real man on earth, did not retain an automatic memory and consciousness. We see the decapitated body of the frog or the cock moving and acting for a time with a seeming intelligence, and why is it not possible for the finer and more subtle astral form to act and move with a far greater amount of seeming mental direction?

Existing in the sphere of *kama loka,* as, indeed, also in all parts of the globe and the solar system, are the elementals or nature forces. They are innumerable, and their divisions are almost infinite, as they are, in a sense, the nerves of nature. Each class has its own work just as has every natural element or thing. As fire burns and as water runs down and not up under their general law, so the elementals act under law, but being higher in the scale than gross fire or water their action seems guided by mind. Some of them have a special relation to mental operations and to the action of the astral organs, whether these be joined to a body or not. When a medium forms the channel, and also from other natural coordination, these elementals make an artificial connection with the shell of a deceased person, aided by the nervous fluid of the medium and others near, and then the shell is galvanized into an artificial life. Through the medium connection is made with the physical and psychical forces of all present. The old impressions on the astral body give up their images to the mind of the medium, the old passions are set on fire. Various messages and reports are then obtained from it, but not one of them is original, not one is from the spirit. By their strangeness, and in consequence of the ignorance of those who dabble in it, this is mistaken for the work of spirit, but it is all from the living when it is not the mere picking out from the astral light of the images of what has been in the past. In certain cases to be noted there is an intelligence at work that is wholly and intensely bad, to which every medium is subject, and which will explain why so many of them have succumbed to evil, as they have confessed.

A rough classification of these shells that visit mediums would be as follows:

(1) Those of the recently deceased whose place of burial is not far away. This class will be quite coherent in accordance with the life and thought of the former owner. An unmaterial, good, and spiritualized person leaves a shell that will soon disintegrate. A gross, mean, selfish, material person's shell will be heavy, consistent, and long lived: and so on with all varieties.

(2) Those of persons who had died far away from the place where the medium is. Lapse of time permits such to escape from the vicinity of their old bodies, and at the same time brings on a greater degree of disintegration which corresponds on the astral plane to putrefaction on the physical. These are vague, shadowy, incoherent; respond

but briefly to the psychic stimulus, and are whirled off by any magnetic current. They are galvanized for a moment by the astral currents of the medium and of those persons present who were related to the deceased.

(3) Purely shadowy remains which can hardly be given a place. There is no English to describe them, though they are facts in this sphere. They might be said to be the mere mold or impress left in the astral substance by the once coherent shell long since disintegrated. They are therefore so near being fictitious as to almost deserve the designation. As such shadowy photographs they are enlarged, decorated, and given an imaginary life by the thoughts, desires, hopes, and imaginings of medium and sitters at the *séance.*

(4) Definite, coherent entities, human souls bereft of thc spiritual tie, now tending down to the worst state of all, *avichi,* where annihilation of the personality is the end. They are known as black magicians. Having centered the consciousness in the principle of *kama,* preserved intellect, divorced themselves from spirit, they are the only damned beings we know. In life they had human bodies and reached their awful state by persistent lives of evil for its own sake; some of such already doomed to become what I have described, are among us on earth today. These are not ordinary shells, for they have centered all their force in *kama,* thrown out every spark of good thought or aspiration, and have a complete mastery of the astral sphere. I put them in the classification of shells because they are such in the sense that they are doomed to disintegration consciously as the others are to the same end mechanically only. They may and do last for many centuries, gratifying their lusts through any sensitive they can lay hold of where

bad thought gives them an opening. They preside at nearly all *séances,* assuming high names and taking the direction so as to keep the control and continue the delusion of the medium, thus enabling themselves to have a convenient channel for their own evil purposes. Indeed, with the shells of suicides, of those poor wretches who die at the hand of the law, of drunkards and gluttons, these black magicians living in the astral world hold the field of physical mediumship and are liable to invade the sphere of any medium no matter how good. The door once open, it is open to all. This class of shell has lost higher *manas,* but in the struggle not only after death but as well in life the lower portion of *manas* which should have been raised up to godlike excellence was torn away from its lord and now gives this entity intelligence which is devoid of spirit but power to suffer as it will when its final day shall come.

In the state of *Kama Loka* suicides and those who are suddenly shot out of life by accident or murder, legal or illegal, pass a term almost equal to the length life would have been but for the sudden termination. These are not really dead. To bring on a normal death, a factor not recognized by medical science must be present. That is, the principles of the being as described in other chapters have their own term of cohesion, at the natural end of which they separate from each other under their own laws. This involves the great subject of the cohesive forces of the human subject, requiring a book in itself. I must be content therefore with the assertion that this law of cohesion obtains among the human principles. Before that natural end the principles are unable to separate. Obviously the normal destruction of the cohesive force cannot be brought about by mechanical processes except in respect to the physical body. Hence a suicide, or person killed by accident or murdered by man or by order of human law, has not come to the natural termination of the cohesion among the other constituents, and is hurled into the *kama loka* state only partly dead. There the remaining principles have to wait until the actual natural life term is reached, whether it be one month or sixty years.

But the degrees of *kama loka* provide for the many varieties of the last-mentioned shells. Some pass the period in great suffering, others in a dreamy sort of sleep, each according to the moral responsibility. But executed criminals are in general thrown out of life full of hate and revenge, smarting under a penalty they do not admit the justice of. They are ever rehearsing in *kama loka* their crime, their trial, their execution, and their revenge. And whenever they can gain touch with a sensitive living person, medium or not, they attempt to inject thoughts of murder and other crime into the brain of such unfortunate. And that they succeed in such attempts the deeper students of Theosophy full well know.

We have now approached *devachan.* After a certain time in *kama loka* the being falls into a state of unconsciousness which precedes the change into the next state. It is like the birth into life, preluded by a term of darkness and heavy sleep. It then wakes to the joys of *devachan.*

CHAPTER XIII
Devachan

HAVING shown that just beyond the threshold of human life there is a place of separation wherein the better part of man is divided from his lower and brute elements, we come to consider what is the state after death of the real being, the immortal who travels from life to life. Struggling out of the body the entire man goes into *kama loka*, to purgatory, where he again struggles and loosens himself from the lower *skandhas*; this period of birth over, the higher principles, *Atma-Buddhi-Manas*, begin to think in a manner different from that which the body and brain permitted in life. This is the state of *Devachan*, a Sanskrit word meaning literally "the place of the gods," where the soul enjoys felicity; but as the gods have no such bodies as ours, the Self in *devachan* is devoid of a mortal body. In the ancient books it is said that this state lasts "for years of infinite number," or "for a period proportionate to the merit of the being"; and when the mental forces peculiar to the state are exhausted, "the being is drawn down again to be reborn in the world of mortals." *Devachan* is therefore an interlude between births in the world. The law of karma which forces us all to enter the world, being ceaseless in its operation and also universal in scope, acts also on the being in *devachan*, for only by the force or operation of Karma are we taken out of *devachan*. It is something like the pressure of atmosphere which, being continuous and uniform, will push out or crush that which is subjected to it unless there be a compensating quantity of atmosphere to counteract the pressure. In the present case the karma of the being is the atmosphere always pressing the being on or out from state to state; the counteracting quantity of atmosphere is the force of the being's own life-thoughts and aspirations which prevent his coming out of *devachan* until that force is exhausted, but which being spent has no more power to hold back the decree of our self-made mortal destiny.

The necessity for this state after death is one of the necessities of evolution growing out of the nature of mind and soul. The very nature of *manas* requires a devachanic state as soon as the body is lost, and it is simply the effect of loosening the bonds placed upon the mind by its physical and astral encasement. In life we can but to a fractional extent act out the thoughts we have each moment; and still less can we exhaust the psychic energies engendered by each day's aspirations and dreams. The energy thus engendered is not lost or annihilated, but is stored in *Manas*, but the body, brain, and astral body permit no full development of the force. Hence, held latent until death, it bursts then from the weakened bonds and plunges *Manas*, the thinker, into the expansion, use, and development of the thought-force set up in life. The impossibility of escaping this necessary state lies in man's ignorance of his own powers and faculties. From this ignorance delusion arises, and *Manas* not being wholly free is carried by its own force into the thinking of *devachan*. But while ignorance is the cause for going into this state the whole process is remedial, restful, and beneficial. For if the average man returned at once to another body in the same civilization he had just quitted, his soul would be completely tired out and deprived of the needed opportunity for the development of the higher part of his nature.

Now the Ego being minus mortal body and *kama*, clothes itself in *devachan* with a vesture which cannot be called body but may be styled means or vehicle, and in that it functions in the devachanic state entirely on the plane of mind and soul. Everything is as real then to the being as this world seems to be to us. It simply now has gotten the opportunity to make its own world for itself unhampered by the clogs of physical life. Its state may be compared to that of the poet or artist who, rapt in ecstacy of composition or arrangement of color, cares not for and knows not of either time or objects of the world.

We are making causes every moment, and but two fields exist for the manifestation in effect of those causes. These are, the objective as this world is called, and the subjective which is both here and after we have left this life. The objective field relates to earth life and the grosser part of man, to his bodily acts and his brain thoughts, as also sometimes to his astral body. The subjective has to do with his higher and spiritual parts. In the objective field the psychic impulses cannot work out, nor can the high leanings and aspirations of his soul; hence these must be the basis, cause, substratum, and support for the state of *devachan.* What then is the time, measured by mortal years, that one will stay in *devachan*?

This question while dealing with what earth-men call time does not, of course, touch the real meaning of time itself, that is, of what may be in fact for this solar system the ultimate order, precedence, succession, and length of moments. It is a question which may be answered in respect to our time, but not certainly in respect to the time on the planet Mercury, for instance, where time is not the same as ours, nor, indeed, in respect to time as conceived by the soul. As to the latter any man can see that after many years have slipped away he has no direct perception of the time just passed, but is able only to pick out some of the incidents which marked its passage, and as to some poignant or happy instants or hours he seems to feel them as but of yesterday. And thus it is for the being in *devachan.* No time is there. The soul has all the benefit of what goes on within itself in that state, but it indulges in no speculations as to the lapse of moments; all is made up of events, while all the time the solar orb is marking off the years for us on the earth plane. This cannot be regarded as an impossibility if we will remember how, as is well known in life, events, pictures, thoughts, argument, introspective feeling will all sweep over us in perfect detail in an instant, or, as is known of those who have been drowning, the events of a whole life time pass in a flash before the eye of the mind. But the Ego remains as said in *devachan* for a time exactly proportioned to the psychic impulses generated during life. Now this being a matter which deals with the mathematics of the soul, no one but a Master can tell what the time would be for the average man of this century in every land. Hence we have to depend on the Masters of wisdom for that average, as it must be based upon a calculation. They have said, as is well put by Mr. A. P. Sinnett in his *Esoteric Buddhism,* that the period is fifteen hundred years in general. From a reading of his book, which was made up from letters from the Masters, it is to be inferred he desires it to be understood that the devachanic period is in each and every case fifteen centuries; but to do away with that misapprehension his informants wrote at a later date that that is the average period and not a fixed one. Such must be the truth, for as we see that men differ in respect to the periods of time they remain in any state of mind in life due to the varying intensities of their thoughts, so it must be in *devachan* where thought has a greater force though always due to the being who had the thoughts.

What the Master did say on this is as follows: The "dream of *devachan*" lasts until karma is satisfied in that direction. In *devachan* there is a "gradual exhaustion of force." "The stay in Devachan is proportioned to the unfinished psychic impulses originating in earth-life: those whose attractions were preponderatingly material will sooner be drawn back into rebirth by the force of *Tanha*." *Tanha* is the thirst for life. He therefore who has not in life originated many psychic impulses will have but little basis or force in his essential nature to keep his higher principles in *devachan*. About all he will have are those originated in childhood before he began to fix his thoughts on materialistic thinking. The thirst for life expressed by the word *Tanha* is the pulling or magnetic force lodged in the *skandhas* inherent in all beings. In such a case as this the average rule does not apply, since the whole effect either way is due to a balancing of forces and is the outcome of action and reaction. And this sort of materialistic thinker may emerge out of *devachan* into another body here in a month, allowing for the unexpended psychic forces originated in early life. But as every one of such persons varies as to class, intensity and quantity of thought and psychic impulse, each may vary in respect to the time of stay in *devachan.* Desperately materialistic thinkers will remain in the devachanic condition stupefied or asleep, as it were, as they have no forces in them appropriate to that state save in a very vague fashion, and for them it can be very truly said that there is no state after death so far as mind is concerned; they are torpid for a while, and then they live again on earth. This general average of the stay in *devachan* gives us the length of a very important human cycle, the Cycle of Reincarnation. For under that law national development will be found to repeat itself, and the times that are past will be found to come again.

The last series of powerful and deeply imprinted thoughts are those which give color and trend to the whole life in *devachan.* The last moment will color each subsequent moment. On those the soul and mind fix themselves and weave of them a whole set of events and experiences, expanding them to their highest limit, carrying out all that was not possible in life. Thus expanding and weaving these thoughts the entity has its youth and growth and growing old, that is, the uprush of the force, its expansion, and its dying down to final exhaustion. If the person has led a colorless life the *devachan* will be colorless; if a rich life, then it will be rich in variety and effect. Existence there is not a dream save in a conventional sense, for it is a stage of the life of man, and when we are there this present life is a dream. It is not in any sense monotonous. We are too prone to measure all possible states of life and places for experience by our present earthly one and to imagine it to be reality. But the life of the soul is endless and not to be stopped for one instant. Leaving our physical body is but a transition to another place or plane for living in. But as the ethereal garments of *devachan* are more lasting than those we wear here, the spiritual, moral, and psychic causes use more time in expanding and exhausting in that state than they do on earth. If the molecules that form the physical body were not subject to the general chemical laws that govern physical earth, then we should live as long in these bodies as we do in the devachanic state. But such a life of endless strain and suffering would be enough to blast the soul compelled to undergo it. Pleasure would then be pain, and surfeit would end but in an immortal insanity. Nature, always kind, leads us soon again into heaven for a rest, for the flowering of the best and highest in our natures.

Devachan is then neither meaningless nor useless. "In it we are rested; that part of us which could not bloom under the chilling skies of earth-life bursts forth into flower and goes back with us to another life stronger and more a part of our nature than before; . . . Why shall we repine that nature kindly aids us in the interminable struggle; why thus keep the mind revolving about this petty personality and its good or evil fortune?"*

But it is sometimes asked, what of those we have left behind: do we see them there? We do not see them there in fact, but we make to ourselves their images as full, complete, and objective as in life, and devoid of all that we then thought was a blemish. We live with them and see them grow great and good instead of mean or bad. The mother who has left a drunken son behind finds him before her in

*Letter from Mahatma K. H. See *Path*, p. 192, Vol. 5.

devachan a sober, good man, and likewise through all possible cases, parent, child, husband, and wife have their loved ones there perfect and full of knowledge. This is for the benefit of the soul. You may call it a delusion if you will, but the illusion is necessary to happiness just as it often is in life. And as it is the mind that makes the illusion, it is no cheat. Certainly the idea of a heaven built over the verge of hell where you must know, if any brains or memory are left to you under the modern orthodox scheme, that your erring friends and relatives are suffering eternal torture, will bear no comparison with the doctrine of *devachan.* But entities in *devachan* are not wholly devoid of power to help those left on earth. Love, the master of life, if real, pure, and deep, will sometimes cause the happy Ego in *devachan* to affect those left on earth for their good, not only in the moral field but also in that of material circumstance. This is possible under a law of the occult universe which cannot be explained now with profit, but the fact may be stated. It has been given out before this by H. P. Blavatsky, without, however, much attention being drawn to it.

The last question to consider is whether we here can reach those in *devachan* or do they come here. We cannot reach them nor affect them unless we are Adepts. The claim of mediums to hold communion with the spirits of the dead is baseless, and still less valid is the claim of ability to help those who have gone to *devachan.* The Mahatma, a being who has developed all his powers and is free from illusion, can go into the devachanic state and then communicate with the Egos there. Such is one of their functions, and that is the only school of the Apostles after death. They deal with certain entities in *devachan* for the purpose of getting them out of the state so as to return to earth for the benefit of the race. The Egos they thus deal with are those whose nature is great and deep but who are not wise enough to be able to overcome the natural illusions of *devachan.* Sometimes also the hypersensitive and pure medium goes into this state and then holds communication with the Egos there, but it is rare, and certainly will not take place with the general run of mediums who trade for money. But the soul never descends here to the medium. And the gulf between the consciousness of *devachan* and that of earth is so deep and wide that it is but seldom the medium can remember upon returning to recollection here what or whom it met or saw or heard in *devachan.* This gulf is similar to that which separates *devachan* from rebirth; it is one in which all memory of what preceded it is blotted out.

The whole period allotted by the soul's forces being ended in *devachan,* the magnetic threads which bind it to earth begin to assert their power. The Self wakes from the dream, it is borne swiftly off to a new body, and then, just before birth, it sees for a moment all the causes that led it to *devachan* and back to the life it is about to begin, and knowing it to be all just, to be the result of its own past life, it repines not but takes up the cross again — and another soul has come back to earth.

CHAPTER XIV
Cycles

THE doctrine of Cycles is one of the most important in the whole theosophical system, though the least known and of all the one most infrequently referred to. Western investigators have for some centuries suspected that events move in cycles, and a few of the writers in the field of European literature have dealt with the subject, but all in a very incomplete fashion. This incompleteness and want of accurate knowledge have been due to the lack of belief in spiritual things and the desire to square everything with materialistic science. Nor do I pretend to give the cyclic law in full, for it is one that is not given out in detail by the Masters of Wisdom. But enough has been divulged, and enough was for a long time known to the Ancients to add considerably to our knowledge.

A cycle is a ring or turning, as the derivation of the word indicates. The corresponding words in the Sanskrit are *Yuga*, *Kalpa*, *Manvantara*, but of these *yuga* comes nearest to cycle, as it is lesser in duration than the others. The beginning of a cycle must be a moment, that added to other moments makes a day, and those added together constitute months, years, decades, and centuries. Beyond this the West hardly goes. It recognizes the moon cycle and the great sidereal one, but looks at both and upon the others merely as periods of time. If we are to consider them as but lengths of time there is no profit except to the dry student or to the astronomer. And in this way today they are regarded by European and American thinkers, who say cycles exist but have no very great bearing on human life and certainly no bearing on the actual recurrence of events or the reappearance on the stage of life of persons who once lived in the world. The theosophical theory is distinctly otherwise, as it must be if it carries out the doctrine of reincarnation to which in preceding pages a good deal of attention has been given. Not only are the cycles named actual physical facts in respect to time, but they and other periods have a very great effect on human life and the evolution of the globe with all the forms of life thereon. Starting with the moment and proceeding through a day, this theory erects the cycle into a comprehensive ring which includes all in its limits. The moment being the basis, the question to be settled in respect to the great cycles is, When did the first moment come? This cannot be answered, but it can be said that the truth is held by the ancient theosophists to be that at the first moments of the solidification of this globe the mass of matter involved attained a certain and definite rate of vibration which will hold through all variations in any part of it until its hour for dissolution comes. These rates of vibration are what determine the different cycles, and, contrary to the ideas of western science, the doctrine is that the solar system and the globe we are now on will come to an end when the force behind the whole mass of seen and unseen matter has reached its limit of duration under cyclic law. Here our doctrine is again different from both the religious and scientific one. We do not admit that the ending of the force is the withdrawal by a God of his protection, nor the sudden propulsion by him of another force against the globe, but that the force at work and determining the great cycle is that of man himself considered as a spiritual being; when he is done using the globe he leaves it, and then with him goes out the force holding all together; the consequence is dissolution by fire or water or what not, these phenomena being simply effects and not causes. The ordinary scientific speculations on this head are that the earth may fall into the sun, or that a comet of density may destroy the globe, or that we may collide with a greater planet known or unknown. These dreams are idle for the present.

Reincarnation being the great law of life and progress, it is interwoven with that of the cycles and karma. These three work together, and in practice it is almost impossible to disentangle reincarnation from cyclic law. Individuals and nations in definite streams return in regularly recurring periods to the earth, and thus bring back to the globe the arts, the civilization, the very persons who once were on it at work. And as the units in nation and race are connected together by invisible strong threads, large bodies of such units moving slowly but surely all together reunite at different times and emerge again and again together into new race and new civilization as the cycles roll their appointed rounds. Therefore the souls who made the most ancient civilizations will come back and bring the old civilization with them in idea and essence, which being added to what others have done for the development of the human race in its character and knowledge will produce a new and higher state of civilization. This newer and better development will not be due to books, to records, to arts or mechanics, because all those are periodically destroyed so far as physical evidence goes, but the soul ever retaining in *Manas* the knowledge it once gained and always pushing to completer development the higher principles and powers, the essence of progress remains and will as surely come out as the sun shines. And along this road are the points when the small and large cycles of Avatars bring out for man's benefit the great characters who mold the race from time to time.

The Cycle of Avatars includes several smaller ones. The greater are those marked by the appearance of Rama and Krishna among the Hindus, of Menes among the Egyptians, of Zoroaster among the Persians, and of Buddha to the Hindus and other nations of the East. Buddha is the last of the great Avatars and is in a larger cycle than is Jesus of the Jews, for the teachings of the latter are the same as those of Buddha and tinctured with what Buddha had taught to those who instructed Jesus. Another great Avatar is yet to come, corresponding to Buddha and Krishna combined. Krishna and Rama were of the military, civil, religious, and occult order; Buddha of the ethical, religious, and mystical, in which he was followed by Jesus; Mohammed was a minor intermediate one for a certain part of the race, and was civil, military, and religious. In these cycles we can include mixed characters who have had great influence on nations, such as King Arthur, Pharaoh, Moses, Charlemagne reincarnated as Napoleon Bonaparte, Clovis of France reborn as Emperor Frederic III of Germany, and Washington the first President of the United States of America where the root for the new race is being formed.

CHAPTER XIV

At the intersection of the great cycles dynamic effects follow and alter the surface of the planet by reason of the shifting of the poles of the globe or other convulsion. This is not a theory generally acceptable, but we hold it to be true. Man is a great dynamo, making, storing, and throwing out energy, and when masses of men composing a race thus make and distribute energy, there is a resulting dynamic effect on the material of the globe which will be powerful enough to be distinct and cataclysmic. That there have been vast and awful disturbances in the strata of the world is admitted on every hand and now needs no proof; these have been due to earthquakes and ice formation so far as concerns geology; but in respect to animal forms the cyclic law is that certain animal forms now extinct and also certain human ones not known but sometimes suspected will return again in their own cycle; and certain human languages now known as dead will be in use once more at their appointed cyclic hour.

"The Metonic cycle is that of the Moon. It is a period of about nineteen years, which being completed the new and the full moons return on the same days of the month."

"The cycle of the Sun is a period of twenty eight years, which having elapsed the Dominical or Sunday letters return to their former place and proceed in the former order according to the Julian calendar."

The great Sidereal year is the period taken by the equinoctial points to make in their precession a complete revolution of the heavens. It is composed of 25,868 solar years almost. It is said that the last sidereal year ended about 9,868 years ago, at which time there must have been on this earth a violent convulsion or series of such, as well as distributions of nations. The completion of this grand period brings the earth into newer spaces of the cosmos, not in respect to its own orbit, but by reason of the actual progress of the sun in an orbit of its own that cannot be measured by any observer of the present day, but which is guessed at by some and located in one of the constellations.

Affecting man especially are the spiritual, psychic, and moral cycles, and out of these grow the national, racial, and individual cycles. Race and national cycles are both historical. The individual cycles are of reincarnation, of sensation, and of impression. The length of the individual reincarnation cycle for the general mass of men is fifteen hundred years, and this in its turn gives us a large historical cycle related closely to the progress of civilization. For as the masses of persons return from *devachan*, it must follow that the Roman, the Greek, the old Aryan, and other Ages will be seen again and can to a very great extent be plainly traced. But man is also affected by astronomical cycles because he is an integral part of the whole, and these cycles mark the periods when mankind as a whole will undergo a change. In the sacred books of all nations these are often mentioned, and are in the Bible of the Christians, as, for instance, in the story of Jonah in the belly of the whale. This is an absurdity when read as history, but not so as an astronomical cycle. "Jonah" is in the constellations, and when that astronomical point which represents man reaches a point in the Zodiac which is directly opposite the belly of Cetus or the whale on the other side of the circle, by what is known as the process of opposition, then Jonah is said to be in the center of the fish and is "thrown out" at the expiration of the period when that man-point has passed so far along in the Zodiac as to be out of opposition to the whale. Similarly as the same point moves thus through the Zodiac it is brought by opposition into the different constellations that are exactly opposite from century to century while it moves along. During these progresses changes take place among men and on earth exactly signified by the constellations when those are read according to the right rules of symbology. It is not claimed that the conjunction causes the effect, but that ages ago the Masters of Wisdom worked out all the problems in respect to man and found in the heavens the means for knowing the exact dates when events are sure to recur, and then by imprinting in the minds of older nations the symbology of the Zodiac were able to preserve the record and the prophecy. Thus in the same way that a watchmaker can tell the hour by the arrival of the hands or the works of the watch at certain fixed points, the Sages can tell the hour for events by the Zodiacal clock. This is not of course believed today, but it will be well understood in future centuries, and as the nations of the earth have all similar symbols in general for the Zodiac, and as also the records of races long dead have the same, it is not likely that the vandal-spirit of the western nineteenth century will be able to efface this valuable heritage of our evolution. In Egypt the Denderah Zodiac tells the same tale as that one left to us by the old civilization of the American continent, and all of these are from the same source, they are the work of the Sages who come at the beginning of the great human cycle and give to man when he begins his toilsome ascent up the road of development those great symbols and ideas of an astronomical character which will last through all the cycles.

In regard to great cataclysms occurring at the beginning and ending of the great cycles, the main laws governing the effects are those of Karma and Reembodiment, or Reincarnation, proceeding under cyclic rule. Not only is man ruled by these laws, but every atom of matter as well, and the mass of matter is constantly undergoing a change at the same time with man. It must therefore exhibit alterations corresponding to those through which the thinker is going. On the physical plane effects are brought out through the electrical and other fluids acting with the gases on the solids of the globe. At the change of a great cycle they reach what may be termed the exploding point and cause violent convulsions of the following classes: (*a*) Earthquakes, (*b*) Floods, (*c*) Fire, (*d*) Ice.

Earthquakes may be brought on according to this philosophy by two general causes; *first*, subsidence or elevation under the earth-crust due to heat and steam, *second*, electrical and magnetic changes which affect water and earth at the same time. These last have the power to instantaneously make the earth fluidic without melting it, thus causing immense and violent displacements in large or small waves. And this effect is sometimes seen now in earthquake districts when similar electrical causes are at work in a smaller measure.

Floods of general extent are caused by displacement of water from the subsidence or elevation of land, and by those combined with electrical change which induces a copious discharge of moisture. The latter is not a mere emptying of a cloud, but a sudden turning of vast bodies of fluids and solids into water.

Universal fires come on from electrical and magnetic changes in the atmosphere by which the moisture is withdrawn from the air and the latter turned into a fiery mass; and, secondly, by the sudden expansion of the solar magnetic center into seven such centers, thus burning the globe.

Ice cataclysms come on not only from the sudden alteration of the poles but also from lowered temperature due to the alteration of the warm fluid currents in the sea and the hot magnetic currents in the earth, the first being known to science, the latter not. The lower stratum of moisture is suddenly frozen, and vast tracts of land covered in a night with many feet of ice. This can easily happen to the British Isles if the warm currents of the ocean are diverted from its shores.

Both Egyptians and Greeks had their cycles, but in our opinion derived them from the Indian Sages. The Chinese always were a nation of astronomers, and have recorded observations reaching far back of the Christian era, but as they belong to an old race which is doomed to extinction — strange as the assertion may appear — their conclusions will not be correct for the Aryan races. On the coming of the Christian era a heavy pall of darkness fell on the minds of men in the West, and India was for many centuries isolated so as to preserve these great ideas during the mental night of Europe. This isolation was brought about deliberately as a necessary precaution taken by that great Lodge to which I adverted in Chapter I, because its Adepts, knowing the cyclic laws perfectly, wished to preserve philosophy for future generations. As it would be mere pedantry and speculation to discuss the unknown Saros and Naros and other cycles of the Egyptians, I will give the Brahmanical ones, since they tally almost exactly with the correct periods.

A period or exhibition of universal manifestation is called a Brahmarandrha,* that is a complete life of Brahma, and Brahma's life is made of his days and years, which, being cosmical are each of immense duration. His day is as man's 24 odd hours long, his year 360 odd days, the number of his years is 100.

Taking now this globe — since we are concerned with no other — its government and evolution proceed under *Manu* or *man*, and from this is the term *Manvantara* or "between two *Manus*." The course of evolution is divided into four *Yugas* for every race in its own time and way. These *Yugas* do not affect all mankind at one and the same time, as some races are in one of the *Yugas* while others are in a different cycle. The Red Indian, for instance, is in the end of his stone age, while the Aryans are in quite a different state. These four *Yugas* are: *Krita*, or *Satya*, the golden; *Treta*; *Dvapara*; and *Kali* or the black. The present age for the West and India is *Kali Yuga*, especially in respect to moral and spiritual development. The first of these is slow in comparison with the rest, and the present — *Kali* — is very rapid, its motion being accelerated precisely like certain astronomical periods known today in regard to the Moon, but not fully worked out.

*[In *The Path,* Nov., 1893, p. 259, Judge points out that this is a misprint for *Brahmanda.*]

CHAPTER XIV

TABLE

	MORTAL YEARS
360 (odd) mortal days make	1
Krita Yuga has	1,728,000
Treta Yuga has	1,296,000
Dvapara Yuga has	864,000
Kali Yuga has	432,000
Maha Yuga, or the four preceding, has	4,320,000
71 *Maha Yugas* form the reign of one Manu, or	306,720,000
14 *Manus* are	4,294,080,000
Add the dawns or twilights between each *Manu*	25,920,000
These reigns and dawns make 1000 *Maha Yugas,* a *Kalpa,* or Day of *Brahma*	4,320,000,000
Brahma's Night equals his Day, and Day and Night together make	8,640,000,000
360 of these Days make *Brahma's* Year	3,110,400,000,000
100 of these Years make *Brahma's* Life	311,040,000,000,000

The first 5000 years of *Kali Yuga* will end between the years 1897 and 1898. This *Yuga* began about 3102 years before the Christian era, at the time of Krishna's death. As 1897-98 are not far off, the scientific men of today will have an opportunity of seeing whether the close of the five thousand year cycle will be preceded or followed by any convulsions or great changes political, scientific, or physical, or all of these combined. Cyclic changes are now proceeding as year after year the souls from prior civilizations are being incarnated in this period when liberty of thought and action are not so restricted in the West as they have been in the past by dogmatic religious prejudice and bigotry. And at the present time we are in a cycle of transition, when, as a transition period should indicate, everything in philosophy, religion, and society is changing. In a transition period the full and complete figures and rules respecting cycles are not given out to a generation which elevates money above all thoughts and scoffs at the spiritual view of man and nature.

CHAPTER XIV

CHAPTER XV
Missing Links

BETWEEN Science and Theosophy there is a wide gulf, for the present unbridged, on the question of the origin of man and the differentiation of species. The teachers of religion in the West offer on this subject a theory, dogmatically buttressed by an assumed revelation, as impossible as the one put forward by scientific men. And yet the religious expounders are nearer than science to the truth. Under the religious superstition about Adam and Eve is hidden the truth, and in the tales of Cain, Seth, and Noah is vaguely shadowed the real story of the other races of men, Adam being but the representative of one single race. The people who received Cain and gave him a wife were some of those human races which had appeared simultaneously with the one headed by Adam.

The ultimate origin or beginning of man is not to be discovered, although we may know when and from where the men of this globe came. Man never was not. If not on this globe, then on some others, he ever was, and will ever be in existence somewhere in the Cosmos. Ever perfecting and reaching up to the image of the Heavenly Man, he is always becoming. But as the human mind cannot go back to any beginning, we shall start with this globe. Upon this earth and upon the whole chain of globes of which it is a part seven races of men appeared simultaneously, coming over to it from other globes of an older chain. And in respect to this earth — the fourth of this chain — these seven races came simultaneously from another globe of this chain. This appearance of seven races together happens in the first and in part of the second round of the globes. In the second round the seven masses of beings are amalgamated, and their destiny after that is to slowly differentiate during the succeeding rounds until at the seventh round the seven first great races will be once more distinct, as perfect types of the human race as this period of evolution will allow. At the present time the seven races are mixed together, and representatives of all are in the many so-called races of men as classified by our present science. The object of this amalgamation and subsequent differentiation is to give to every race the benefit of the progress and power of the whole derived from prior progress in other planets and systems. For Nature never does her work in a hasty or undue fashion, but, by the sure method of mixture, precipitation, and separation, brings about the greatest perfection. And this method was one known to the Alchemists, though not fully understood in all its bearings even by them.

Hence man did not spring from a single pair. Neither did he come from any tribe or family of monkey. It is hopeless to look to either religion or science for a solution of the question, for science is confused on her own admission, and religion is tangled with a revelation that in its books controverts the theory put forward by the priest. Adam is called the first man, but the record in which the story is found shows that other races of men must have existed on the earth before Cain could have founded a city. The Bible, then, does not support the single pair theory. If we take up one of the hypotheses of Science and admit for the moment that man and monkey differentiated from one ancestor, we have then to decide where the first ancestor came from. The first postulate of the Lodge on this subject is that seven races of men appeared simultaneously on the earth, and the first negative assumption is that man did not spring from a single pair or from the animal kingdom.

The varieties of character and capacity which subsequently appear in man's history are the forthcoming of the variations which were induced in the Egos in other and long anterior periods of evolution upon other chains of globes. These variations were so deeply impacted as to be equivalent to inherent characteristics. For the races of this globe the prior period of evolution was passed on the chain of globes of which our moon is the visible representative.

The burning question of the anthropoid apes as related to man is settled by the Masters of Wisdom, who say that instead of those being our progenitors they were produced by man himself. In one of the early periods of the globe the men of that time begot from large females of the animal kingdom the anthropoids, and in anthropoid bodies were caught a certain number of Egos destined one day to be men. The remainder of the descendants of the true anthropoid are the descendants of those illegitimate children of men, and will die away gradually, their Egos entering human bodies. Those half-ape and half-man bodies could not be ensouled by strictly animal Egos, and for that reason they are known to the Secret Doctrine as the "Delayed Race," the only one not included in the fiat of Nature that no more Egos from the lower kingdoms will come into the human kingdom until the next *Manvantara.* But to all kingdoms below man except the anthropoids, the door is now closed for entry into the human stage, and the Egos in the subordinate forms must all wait their turn in the succeeding great Cycle. And as the delayed Egos of the Anthropoid family will emerge into the man stage later on, they will thus be rewarded for the long wait in that degraded race. All the other monkeys are products in the ordinary manner of the evolutionary processes.

On this subject I cannot do better than quote the words of one of those Masters of Wisdom, giving the esoteric anthropology from the secret volumes, thus:

> The anatomical resemblance between Man and the higher Ape, so frequently cited by Darwinists as pointing to some former ancestor common to both, presents an interesting problem, the proper solution of which is to be sought for in the esoteric explanation of the genesis of the pithecoid stocks. We have given it so far as was useful, by stating that the bestiality of the primeval mindless races resulted in the production of huge man-like monsters — the offspring of human and animal parents. As time rolled on, and the still semi-astral forms consolidated into the physical, the descendants of these creatures were modified by external conditions, until the breed, dwindling in size, culminated in the lower apes of the Miocene period. With these the later Atlanteans renewed the sin of the "Mindless" — this time with full responsibility. The resultants of their crime were the species of apes now known as the Anthropoid. . . .
>
> Let us remember in this connection the esoteric teaching which tells us of Man having had in the Third Round a GIGANTIC APE-LIKE FORM on the astral plane. And similarly at the close of the Third Race in this Round. Thus it accounts for the human features of the Apes, especially of the later Anthropoids, — apart from the fact that these latter preserved by *Heredity* a resemblance to their Atlanto-Lemurian sires.

The same teachers furthermore assert that the mammalian types were produced in the fourth round, subsequent to the appearance of the human types. For this reason there was no barrier against fertility, because the root-types of those mammals were not far enough removed to raise the natural barrier. The unnatural union in the third race, when man had not yet had the light of *Manas* given to him, was not a crime against Nature, since, no mind being present save in the merest germ, no responsibility could attach. But in the fourth round, the light of *Manas* being present, the renewal of the act by the new race was a crime, because it was done with a full knowledge of the consequences and against the warning of conscience. The karmic effect of this, including as it does all races, has yet to be fully felt and understood — at a much later day than now.

As man came to this globe from another planet, though of course then a being of very great power before being completely enmeshed in matter, so the lower kingdoms came likewise in germ and type from other planets, and carry on their evolution step by step upward by the aid of man, who is, in all periods of manifestation, at the front of the wave of life. The Egos in these lower kingdoms could not finish their evolution in the preceding globe-chain before its dissolution, and coming to this they go forward age after age, gradually approaching nearer the man stage. One day they too will become men and act as the advance guard and guide for other lower kingdoms of this or other globes. And in the coming from the former planet there are always brought with the first and highest class of beings some forms of animal life, some fruits and other products, as models or types for use here. It will not be profitable to go into this here with particularity, for being too far ahead of the time it would evoke only ridicule from some and stupidity from others. But the general forms of the various kingdoms being so brought over, we have next to consider how the differentiation of animal and other lower species began and was carried on.

This is the point where intelligent aid and interference from a mind or mass of minds is absolutely necessary. Such aid and interference was and is the fact, for Nature unaided cannot do the work right. But I do not mean that God or angel interferes and aids. It is Man who does this. Not the man of the day, weak and ignorant as he is, but great souls, high and holy men of immense power, knowledge, and wisdom. Just such as every man would now know he could become, if it were not that religion on one hand and science on the other have painted such a picture of our weakness, inherent evil and purely material origin that nearly all men think they are puppets of God or cruel fate without hope, or remain with a degrading and selfish aim in view both here and after. Various names have been given to these beings now removed from our plane. They are the *Dhyanis,* the Creators, the Guides, the Great Spirits, and so on by many titles. In theosophical literature they are called the *Dhyanis.*

By methods known to themselves and to the Great Lodge they work on the forms so brought over, and by adding here, taking away there, and often altering, they gradually transform by such alteration and addition the kingdoms of nature as well as the gradually forming gross body of man. This process is carried on chiefly in the purely astral period preceding the gross physical stage, as the impulses thus given will surely carry themselves forward through the succeeding times. When the midway point of evolution is reached the species emerge on to the present stage and not showing the connection to the eye of man nor to our instruments. The investigations of the day have traced certain species down to a point where, as is confessed, it is not known to what root they go back. Taking oxen on one side and horses on the other, we see that both are hoofed, but one has a split hoof and the other but one toe. These bring us back, when we reach the oldest ancestor of each, to the midway point, and there science has to stop. At this spot the wisdom of the Masters comes in to show that back of this is the astral region of ancient evolution, where were the root-types in which the Dhyanis began the evolution by alteration and addition which resulted in the differentiation afterwards on this gross plane into the various families, species, and genera.

A vast period of time, about 300,000,000 years, was passed by earth and man and all the kingdoms of nature in an astral stage. Then there was no gross matter such as we now know. This was in the early rounds when Nature was proceeding slowly with the work of perfecting the types on the astral plane, which is matter, though very fine in its texture. At the end of that stretch of years the process of hardening began, the form of man being the first to become solid, and then some of the astral prototypes of the preceding rounds were involved in the solidification, though really belonging to a former period when everything was astral. When those fossils are discovered it is argued that they must be those of creatures which co-existed with the gross physical body of man.

While that argument is proper enough under the other theories of Science, it becomes only an assumption if the existence of the astral period be admitted. It would be beyond the scope of this work to go further into particulars. But it may incidentally be said that neither the bee nor the wheat could have had their original differentiation in this chain of globes, but must have been produced and finished in some other from which they were brought over into this. Why this should be so I am willing to leave for the present to conjecture.

To the whole theory it may be objected that Science has not been able to find the missing links between the root-types of the astral period and the present fossils or living species. In the year 1893 at Moscow Professor Virchow said in a lecture that the missing link was as far off as ever, as much of a dream as ever, and that no real evidence was at hand to show man as coming from the animals. This is quite true, and neither class of missing link will be discovered by Science under her present methods. For all of them exist in the astral plane and therefore are invisible to the physical eye. They can only be seen by the inner astral senses, which must first be trained to do their work properly, and until Science admits the existence of the astral and inner senses she will never try to develop them. Always, then, Science will be without the instruments for discovering the astral links left on the astral plane in the long course of differentiation. The fossils spoken of above, which were, so to say, solidified out of date, form an exception to the impossibility of finding any missing links, but they are blind alleys to Science because she admits none of the necessary facts.

The object of all this differentiation, amalgamation, and separation is well stated by another of the Masters, thus:

> Nature consciously prefers that matter should be indestructible under organic rather than under inorganic forms; and that she works slowly but incessantly towards the realization of this object — the evolution of conscious life out of inert material.

CHAPTER XV

CHAPTER XVI
Psychic Laws and Forces

THE field of psychic forces, phenomena, and dynamics is a vast one. Such phenomena are seen and the forces exhibited every day in all lands, but until a few years ago very little attention was given to them by scientific persons, while a great deal of ridicule was heaped upon those who related the occurrences or averred belief in the psychic nature. A cult sprang up in the United States some forty years ago calling itself quite wrongly "spiritualism," but having a great opportunity it neglected it and fell into mere wonder-seeking without the slightest shadow of a philosophy. It has accomplished but little in the way of progress except a record of many undigested facts which for four decades failed to attract the serious attention of people in general. While it has had its uses, and includes in its ranks many good minds, the great dangers and damages coming to the human instruments involved and to those who sought them more than offset the good done in the opinion of those disciples of the Lodge who would have man progress evenly and without ruin along his path of evolution. But other Western investigators of the accepted schools have not done much better, and the result is that there is no Western Psychology worthy of the name.

This lack of an adequate system of Psychology is a natural consequence of the materialistic bias of science and the paralyzing influence of dogmatic religion; the one ridiculing effort and blocking the way, the other forbidding investigation. The Roman Catholic branch of the Christian Church is in some respects an exception, however. It has always admitted the existence of the psychic world — for it the realm of devils and angels, but as angels manifest when they choose and devils are to be shunned, no one is permitted by that Church to meddle in such matters except an authorized priest. So far as that Church's prohibiting the pernicious practice of necromancy indulged in by "spiritualists" it was right, but not in its other prohibitions and restrictions. Real psychology is an Oriental product today. Very true the system was known in the West when a very ancient civilization flourished in America, and in certain parts of Europe anterior to the Christian era, but for the present day psychology in its true phase belongs to the Orient.

Are there psychic forces, laws, and powers? If there are, then there must be the phenomena. And if all that has been outlined in preceding chapters is true, then in man are the same powers and forces which are to be found anywhere in Nature. He is held by the Masters of Wisdom to be the highest product of the whole system of evolution, and mirrors in himself every power, however wonderful or terrible, of Nature; by the very fact of being such a mirror he is man.

This has long been recognized in the East, where the writer has seen exhibitions of such powers which would upset the theories of many a Western man of science. And in the West the same phenomena have been repeated for the writer, so that he knows of his own knowledge that every man of every race has the same powers potentially. The genuine psychic — or, as they are often called, magical

— phenomena done by the Eastern faquir or yogee are all performed by the use of natural forces and processes not even dreamed of as yet by the West. Levitation of the body in apparent defiance of gravitation is a thing to be done with ease when the process is completely mastered. It contravenes no law. Gravitation is only half of a law. The Oriental sage admits gravity, if one wishes to adopt the term; but the real term is attraction, the other half of the law being expressed by the word repulsion, and both being governed by the great laws of electrical force. Weight and stability depend on polarity, and when the polarity of an object is altered in respect to the earth immediately underneath it, then the object may rise. But as mere objects are devoid of the consciousness found in man, they cannot rise without certain other aids. The human body, however, will rise in the air unsupported, like a bird, when its polarity is thus changed. This change is brought about consciously by a certain system of breathing known to the Oriental; it may be induced also by aid from certain natural forces spoken of later, in the cases of those who without knowing the law perform the phenomena, as with the saints of the Roman Catholic Church.

A third great law which enters into many of the phenomena of the East and West is that of Cohesion. The power of Cohesion is a distinct power of itself, and not a result as is supposed. This law and its action must be known if certain phenomena are to be brought about, as, for instance, what the writer has seen, the passing of one solid iron ring through another, or a stone through a solid wall. Hence another force is used which can only be called dispersion. Cohesion is the dominating force, for, the moment the dispersing force is withdrawn, the cohesive force restores the particles to their original position.

Following this out the Adept in such great dynamics is able to disperse the atoms of an object — excluding always the human body — to such a distance from each other as to render the object invisible, and then can send them along a current formed in the ether to any distance on the earth. At the desired point the dispersing force is withdrawn, when immediately cohesion reasserts itself and the object reappears intact. This may sound like fiction, but being known to the Lodge and its disciples as an actual fact, it is equally certain that Science will sooner or later admit the proposition.

But the lay mind infested by the materialism of the day wonders how all these manipulations are possible, seeing that no instruments are spoken of. The instruments are in the body and brain of man. In the view of the Lodge "the human brain is an exhaustless generator of force," and a complete knowledge of the inner chemical and dynamic laws of Nature, together with a trained mind, give the possessor the power to operate the laws to which I have referred. This will be man's possession in the future, and would be his today were it not for blind dogmatism, selfishness, and materialistic unbelief. Not even the Christian lives up to his Master's very true statement that if one had faith he could remove a mountain. A knowledge of the law when added to faith gives power over matter, mind, space, and time.

Using the same powers, the trained Adept can produce before the eye, objective to the touch, material which was not visible before, and in any desired shape. This would be called creation by the vulgar, but it is simply evolution in your very presence. Matter is held suspended in the air about us. Every particle of matter, visible or still unprecipitated, has been through all possible forms, and what the Adept does is to select any desired form, existing, as they all do, in the Astral Light and then by effort of the Will and Imagination to clothe the form with the matter by precipitation. The object so made will fade away unless certain other processes are resorted to which need not be here described, but if these processes are used the object will remain permanently. And if it is desired to make visible a message on paper or other surface, the same laws and powers are used. The distinct — photographically and sharply definite — image of every line of every letter or picture is formed in the mind, and then out of the air is drawn the pigment to fall within the limits laid down by the brain, "the exhaustless generator of force and form." All these things the writer has seen done in the way described, and not by any hired or irresponsible medium, and he knows whereof he speaks.

This, then, naturally leads to the proposition that the human Will is all powerful and the Imagination is a most useful faculty with a dynamic force. The Imagination is the picture-making power of the human mind. In the ordinary average human person it has not enough training or force to be more than a sort of dream, but it may be trained. When trained it is the Constructor in the Human Workshop. Arrived at that stage it makes a matrix in the Astral substance through which effects objectively will flow. It is the greatest power, after Will, in the human assemblage of complicated instruments. The modern

Western definition of Imagination is incomplete and wide of the mark. It is chiefly used to designate fancy or misconception and at all times stands for unreality. It is impossible to get another term as good because one of the powers of the trained Imagination is that of making an image. The word is derived from those signifying the formation or reflection of an image. This faculty used, or rather suffered to act, in an unregulated mode has given the West no other idea than that covered by "fancy." So far as that goes it is right but it may be pushed to a greater limit, which, when reached causes the Imagination to evolve in the Astral substance an actual image or form which may be then used in the same way as an iron molder uses a mold of sand for the molten iron. It is therefore the King faculty, inasmuch as the Will cannot do its work if the Imagination be at all weak or untrained. For instance, if the person desiring to precipitate from the air wavers in the least with the image made in the Astral substance, the pigment will fall upon the paper in a correspondingly wavering and diffused manner.

To communicate with another mind at any distance the Adept attunes all the molecules of the brain and all the thoughts of the mind so as to vibrate in unison with the mind to be affected, and that other mind and brain have also to be either voluntarily thrown into the same unison or fall into it voluntarily. So though the Adept be at Bombay and his friend in New York, the distance is no obstacle, as the inner senses are not dependent on an ear, but may feel and see the thoughts and images in the mind of the other person.

And when it is desired to look into the mind and catch

the thoughts of another and the pictures all around him of all he has thought and looked at, the Adept's inner sight and hearing are directed to the mind to be seen, when at once all is visible. But, as said before, only a rogue would do this, and the Adepts do not do it except in strictly authorized cases. The modern man sees no misdemeanor in looking into the secrets of another by means of this power, but the Adepts say it is an invasion of the rights of the other person. No man has the right, even when he has the power in his hand, to enter into the mind of another and pick out its secrets. This is the law of the Lodge to all who seek, and if one sees that he is about to discover the secrets of another he must at once withdraw and proceed no further. If he proceeds his power is taken from him in the case of a disciple; in the case of any other person he must take the consequence of this sort of burglary. For Nature has her laws and her policemen, and if we commit felonies in the Astral world the great Law and the guardians of it, for which no bribery is possible, will execute the penalty, no matter how long we wait, even if it be for ten thousand years. Here is another safeguard for ethics and morals. But until men admit the system of philosophy put forward in this book, they will not deem it wrong to commit felonies in fields where their weak human law has no effect, but at the same time by thus refusing the philosophy they will put off the day when all may have these great powers for the use of all.

Among phenomena useful to notice are those consisting of the moving of objects without physical contact. This may be done, and in more than one way. The first is to extrude from the physical body the Astral hand and arm, and with those grasp the object to be moved. This may be accomplished at a distance of as much as ten feet from the person. I do not go into argument on this, only referring to the properties of the Astral substance and members. This will serve to some extent to explain several of the phenomena of mediums. In nearly all cases of such apportation the feat is accomplished by thus using the unseen but material Astral hand. The second method is to use the elementals of which I have spoken. They have the power when directed by the inner man to carry objects by changing the polarity, and then we see, as with the fakirs of India and some mediums in America, small objects moving apparently unsupported. These elemental entities are used when things are brought from longer distances than the length to which the Astral members may be stretched. It is no argument against this that mediums do not know they do so. They rarely if ever know anything about how they accomplish any feat, and their ignorance of the law is no proof of its non-existence. Those students who have seen the forces work from the inside will need no argument on this.

Clairvoyance, clairaudience, and second-sight are all related very closely. Every exercise of any one of them draws in at the same time both of the others. They are but variations of one power. Sound is one of the distinguishing characteristics of the Astral sphere, and as light goes with sound, sight obtains simultaneously with hearing. To see an image with the Astral senses means that at the same time there is a sound, and to hear the latter infers the presence of a related image in Astral substance. It is perfectly well known to the true student of occultism that every sound produces instantaneously an image, and this, so long known in the Orient, has lately been demonstrated in the West in the production to the eye of sound pictures on a stretched tympanum. This part of the subject can be gone into very much further with the aid of occultism, but as it is a dangerous one in the present state of society I refrain at this point. In the Astral Light are pictures of all things whatsoever that happened to any person, and as well also pictures of those events to come the causes for which are sufficiently well marked and made. If the causes are yet indefinite, so will be the images of the future. But for the mass of events for several years to come all the producing and efficient causes are always laid down with enough definiteness to permit the seer to see them in advance as if present. By means of these pictures, seen with the inner senses, all clairvoyants exercise their strange faculty. Yet it is a faculty common to all men, though in the majority but slightly developed; but occultism asserts that were it not for the germ of this power slightly active in every one no man could convey to another any idea whatsoever.

In clairvoyance the pictures in the Astral Light pass before the inner vision and are reflected into the physical eye from within. They then appear objectively to the seer. If they are of past events or those to come, the picture only is seen; if of events actually then occurring, the scene is perceived through the Astral Light by the inner sense. The distinguishing difference between ordinary and clairvoyant vision is, then, that in clairvoyance with waking sight the vibration is communicated to the brain first, from which it is transmitted to the physical eye, where it sets up an image upon the retina, just as the revolving cylinder of the phonograph causes the mouthpiece to vibrate exactly as the voice had vibrated when thrown into the receiver. In ordinary eye vision the vibrations are given to the eye first and then transmitted to the brain. Images and sounds are both caused by vibrations, and hence any sound once made is preserved in the Astral Light from whence the inner sense can take it and from within transmit it to the brain, from which it reaches the physical ear. So in clairaudience at a distance the hearer does not hear with the ear, but with the center of hearing in the Astral body. Second-sight is a combination of clairaudience and clairvoyance or not, just as the particular case is, and the frequency with which future events are seen by the second-sight seer adds an element of prophecy.

The highest order of clairvoyance — that of spiritual vision — is very rare. The usual clairvoyant deals only with the ordinary aspects and strata of the Astral matter. Spiritual sight comes only to those who are pure, devoted, and firm. It may be attained by special development of the particular organ in the body through which alone such sight is possible, and only after discipline, long training, and the highest altruism. All other clairvoyance is transitory, inadequate, and fragmentary, dealing, as it does, only with matter and illusion. Its fragmentary and inadequate character results from the fact that hardly any clairvoyant has the power to see into more than one of the lower grades of Astral substance at any one time. The pure-minded and the brave can deal with the future and the present far better than any clairvoyant. But as the existence of these two powers proves the presence in us of the inner senses and of the necessary medium — the Astral Light, they have, as such human faculties, an important bearing upon the claims made by the so-called "spirits" of the *séance* room.

Dreams are sometimes the result of brain action automatically proceeding, and are also produced by the transmission into the brain by the real inner person of those scenes or ideas high or low which that real person has seen while the body slept. They are then strained into the brain as if floating on the soul as it sinks into the body. These dreams may be of use, but generally the resumption of bodily activity destroys the meaning, perverts the image, and reduces all to confusion. But the great fact of all dreaming is that some one perceives and feels therein, and this is one of the arguments for the inner person's existence. In sleep the inner man communes with higher intelligences, and sometimes succeeds in impressing the brain with what is gained, either a high idea or a prophetic vision, or else fails in consequence of the resistance of brain fiber. The karma of the person also determines the meaning of a dream, for a king may dream that which relates to his kingdom, while the same thing dreamed by a citizen relates to nothing of temporal consequence. But, as said by Job: In dreams and visions of the night man is instructed.

Apparitions and doubles are of two general classes. The one, astral shells or images from the astral world, either actually visible to the eye or the result of vibration within thrown out to the eye and thus making the person think he sees an objective form without. The other, the astral body of living persons and carrying full consciousness or only partially so endowed. Laborious attempts by Psychical Research Societies to prove apparitions without knowing these laws really prove nothing, for out of twenty admitted cases nineteen may be the objectivization of the image impressed on the brain. But that apparitions have been seen there is no doubt. Apparitions of those just dead may be either pictures made objective as described, or the Astral Body — called *Kama Rupa* at this stage — of the deceased. And as the dying thoughts and forces released from the body are very strong, we have more accounts of such apparitions than of any other class.

The Adept may send out his apparition, which, however, is called by another name, as it consists of his conscious and trained astral body endowed with all his intelligence and not wholly detached from his physical frame.

Theosophy does not deny nor ignore the physical laws discovered by science. It admits all such as are proven, but it asserts the existence of others which modify the action of those we ordinarily know. Behind all the visible phenomena is the occult cosmos with its ideal machinery; that occult cosmos can only be fully understood by means of the inner senses which pertain to it; those senses will not be easily developed if their existence is denied. Brain and mind acting together have the power to evolve forms, first as astral ones in astral substance, and later as visible ones by accretions of the matter on this plane. Objectivity depends largely on perception, and perception may be affected by inner stimuli. Hence a witness may either see an object which actually exists as such without, or may be made to see one by internal stimulus.

CHAPTER XVI

This gives us three modes of sight: (*a*) with the eye by means of light from an object, (*b*) with the inner senses by means of the Astral Light, and (*c*) by stimulus from within which causes the eye to report to the brain, thus throwing the inner image without. The phenomena of the other senses may be tabulated in the same manner.

The Astral substance being the register of all thoughts, sounds, pictures, and other vibrations, and the inner man being a complete person able to act with or without co-ordination with the physical, all the phenomena of hypnotism, clairvoyance, clairaudience, mediumship, and the rest of those which are not consciously performed may be explained. In the Astral substance are all sounds and pictures, and in the Astral man remain impressions of every event, however remote or insignificant; these acting together produce the phenomena which seem so strange to those who deny or are unaware of the postulates of occultism.

But to explain the phenomena performed by Adepts, Fakirs, Yogees, and all trained occultists, one has to understand the occult laws of chemistry, of mind, of force, and of matter. These it is obviously not the province of such a work as this to treat in detail.

CHAPTER XVII
Psychic Phenomena and Spiritualism

IN the history of psychical phenomena the records of so-called "spiritualism" in Europe, America, and elsewhere hold an important place. Advisedly I say that no term was ever more misapplied than that of "spiritualism" to the cult in Europe and America just mentioned, inasmuch as there is nothing of the spirit about it. The doctrines given in preceding chapters are those of true spiritualism; the misnamed practises of modern mediums and so-called spiritists constitute the Worship of the Dead, old-fashioned necromancy, in fact, which was always prohibited by spiritual teachers. They are a gross materializing of the spiritual idea, and deal with matter more than with its opposite. This cult is supposed by some to have originated about forty years ago in America at Rochester, N. Y., under the mediumship of the Fox sisters, but it was known in Salem during the witchcraft excitement, and in Europe one hundred years ago the same practises were pursued, similar phenomena seen, mediums developed, and *séances* held. For centuries it has been well known in India where it is properly designated "*bhuta* worship," meaning the attempt to communicate with the devil or Astral remnants of deceased persons. This should be its name here also, for by it the gross and devilish, or earthly, parts of man are excited, appealed to, and communicated with. But the facts of the long record of forty years in America demand a brief examination. These facts all studious Theosophists must admit. The theosophical explanation and deductions, however, are totally different from those of the average spiritualist. A philosophy has not been evolved in the ranks or literature of spiritualism; nothing but theosophy will give the true explanation, point out defects, reveal dangers, and suggest remedies.

As it is plain that clairvoyance, clairaudience, thought-transference, prophecy, dream and vision, levitation, apparitional appearance, are all powers that have been known for ages, the questions most pressing in respect to spiritualism are those relating to communication with the souls of those who have left this earth and are now disembodied, and with unclassified spirits who have not been embodied here but belong to other spheres. Perhaps also the question of materialization of forms at *séances* deserves some attention. Communication includes trance-speaking, slate and other writing, independent voices in the air, speaking through the physical vocal organs of the medium, and precipitation of written messages out of the air. Do the mediums communicate with the spirits of the dead? Do our departed friends perceive the state of life they have left, and do they sometimes return to speak to and with us?

The answers are intimated in foregoing chapters. Our departed do not see us here. They are relieved from the terrible pang such a sight would inflict. Once in a while a pure-minded, unpaid medium may ascend in trance to the state in which a deceased soul is, and may remember some bits of what was there heard; but this is rare. Now and then in the course of decades some high human spirit may for a moment return and by unmistakable means communicate with mortals. At the moment of death the soul may speak to some friend on earth before the door is finally shut. But the mass of communications alleged as made day after day through mediums are from the astral unintelligent remains of men, or in many cases entirely the production of, invention, compilation, discovery, and collocation by the loosely attached Astral body of the living medium.

Certain objections arise to the theory that the spirits of the dead communicate. Some are:

I. At no time have these spirits given the laws governing any of the phenomena, except in a few instances, not accepted by the cult, where the theosophical theory was advanced. As it would destroy such structures as those erected by A. J. Davis, these particular spirits fell into discredit.

II. The spirits disagree among themselves, one stating the after-life to be very different from the description by another. These disagreements vary with the medium and the supposed theories of the deceased during life. One spirit admits reincarnation and others deny it.

III. The spirits have discovered nothing in respect to history, anthropology, or other important matters, seeming to have less ability in that line than living men; and although they often claim to be men who lived in older civilizations, they show ignorance thereupon or merely repeat recently published discoveries.

IV. In these forty years no *rationale* of phenomena nor of development of mediumship has been obtained from the spirits. Great philosophers are reported as speaking through mediums, but utter only drivel and merest commonplaces.

CHAPTER XVII

V. The mediums come to physical and moral grief, are accused of fraud, are shown guilty of trickery, but the spirit guides and controls do not interfere to either prevent or save.

VI. It is admitted that the guides and controls deceive and incite to fraud.

VII. It is plainly to be seen through all that is reported of the spirits that their assertions and philosophy, if any, vary with the medium and the most advanced thought of living spiritualists.

From all this and much more that could be adduced, the man of materialistic science is fortified in his ridicule, but the theosophist has to conclude that the entities, if there be any communicating, are not human spirits, and that the explanations are to be found in some other theories.

Materialization of a form out of the air, independent of the medium's physical body, is a fact. But it is not a spirit. As was very well said by one of the "spirits" not favored by spiritualism, one way to produce this phenomenon is by the accretion of electrical and magnetic particles into one mass upon which matter is aggregated and an image reflected out of the Astral sphere. This is the whole of it; as much a fraud as a collection of muslin and masks. How this is accomplished is another matter. The spirits are not able to tell, but an attempt has been made to indicate the methods and instruments in former chapters. The second method is by the use of the Astral body of the living medium. In this case the Astral form exudes from the side of the medium, gradually collects upon itself particles extracted from the air and the bodies of the sitters present, until at last it becomes visible. Sometimes it will resemble the medium; at others it bears a different appearance. In almost every instance dimness of light is requisite because a high light would disturb the Astral substance in a violent manner and render the projection difficult. Some so-called materializations are hollow mockeries, as they are but flat plates of electrical and magnetic substance on which pictures from the Astral Light are reflected. These seem to be the faces of the dead, but they are simply pictured illusions.

If one is to understand the psychic phenomena found in the history of "spiritualism" it is necessary to know and admit the following:

I. The complete heredity of man astrally, spiritually, and psychically, as a being who knows, reasons, feels, and acts through the body, the Astral body, and the soul.

II. The nature of the mind, its operation, its powers; the nature and power of imagination; the duration and effect of impressions. Most important in this is the persistence of the slightest impression as well as the deepest; that every impression produces a picture in the individual aura; and that by means of this a connection is established between the auras of friends and relatives old, new, near, distant, and remote in degree: this would give a wide range of possible sight to a clairvoyant.

III. The nature, extent, function, and power of man's inner Astral organs and faculties included in the terms Astral body and *Kama.* That these are not hindered from action by trance or sleep, but are increased in the medium when entranced; at the same time their action is not free, but governed by the mass chord of thought among the sitters, or by a predominating will, or by the presiding devil behind the scenes; if a sceptical scientific investigator be present, his mental attitude may totally inhibit the action of the medium's powers by what we might call a freezing process which no English terms will adequately describe.

IV. The fate of the real man after death, his state, power, activity there, and his relation, if any, to those left behind him, here.

V. That the intermediary between mind and body — the Astral body — is thrown off at death and left in the Astral light to fade away; and that the real man goes to *Devachan.*

VI. The existence, nature, power, and function of the Astral light and its place as a register in Nature. That it contains, retains, and reflects pictures of each and every thing that happened to anyone, and also every thought; that it permeates the globe and the atmosphere around it; that the transmission of vibration through it is practically instantaneous, since the rate is much quicker than that of electricity as now known.

VII. The existence in the Astral light of beings not using bodies like ours, but not human in their nature, having powers, faculties, and a sort of consciousness of their own; these include the elemental forces or nature sprites divided into many degrees, and which have to do with every operation of Nature and every motion of the mind of man. That these elementals act at *séances* automatically in their various departments, one class presenting pictures, another producing sounds, and others depolarizing objects for the purposes of apportation. Acting with them in this Astral sphere are the soulless men who live in it. To these are to be ascribed the phenomenon, among others, of the "independent voice," always sounding like a voice in a barrel just because it is made in a vacuum which is absolutely necessary for an entity so far removed from spirit. The peculiar *timbre* of this sort of voice has not been noticed by the spiritualists as important, but it is extremely significant in the view of occultism.

VIII. The existence and operation of occult laws and forces in nature which may be used to produce phenomenal results on this plane; that these laws and forces may be put into operation by the subconscious man and by the elementals either consciously or unconsciously, and that many of these occult operations are automatic in the same way as is the freezing of water under intense cold or the melting of ice under heat.

IX. That the Astral body of the medium, partaking of the nature of the Astral substance, may be extended from the physical body, may act outside of the latter, and may also extrude at times any portion of itself such as hand, arm, or leg and thereby move objects, indite letters, produce touches on the body, and so on *ad infinitum.* And that the Astral body of any person may be made to feel sensation, which, being transmitted to the brain, causes the person to think he is touched on the outside or has heard a sound.

Mediumship is full of dangers because the Astral part of the man is now only normal in action when joined to the body; in distant years it will normally act without a body as it has in the far past. To become a medium means that you have to become disorganized physiologically and in the nervous system, because through the latter is the connection between the two worlds. The moment the door is opened all the unknown forces rush in, and as the grosser part of nature is nearest to us it is that part which affects us most; the lower nature is also first affected and inflamed because the forces used are from that part of us. We are then at the mercy of the vile thoughts of all men, and subject to the influence of the shells in *Kama Loka.* If to this be added the taking of money for the practice of mediumship, an additional danger is at hand, for the things of the spirit and those relating to the Astral world must not be sold. This is the great disease of American spiritualism which has debased and degraded its whole history; until it is eliminated no good will come from the practice; those who wish to hear truth from the other world must devote themselves to truth and leave all considerations of money out of sight.

To attempt to acquire the use of the psychic powers for mere curiosity or for selfish ends is also dangerous for the same reasons as in the case of mediumship. As the civilization of the present day is selfish to the last degree and built on the personal element, the rules for the development of these powers in the right way have not been given out, but the Masters of Wisdom have said that philosophy and ethics must first be learned and practiced before any development of the other department is to be indulged in; and their condemnation of the wholesale development of mediums is supported by the history of spiritualism, which is one long story of the ruin of mediums in every direction.

Equally improper is the manner of the scientific schools which without a thought for the true nature of man indulge in experiments in hypnotism in which the subjects are injured for life, put into disgraceful attitudes, and made to do things for the satisfaction of the investigators which would never be done by men and women in their normal state. The Lodge of the Masters does not care for Science unless it aims to better man's state morally as well as physically, and no aid will be given to Science until she looks at man and life from the moral and spiritual side. For this reason those who know all about the psychical world, its denizens and laws, are proceeding with a reform in morals and philosophy before any great attention will be accorded to the strange and seductive phenomena possible for the inner powers of man.

And at the present time the cycle has almost run its course for this century. Now, as a century ago, the forces are slackening; for that reason the phenomena of spiritualism are lessening in number and volume; the Lodge hopes by the time the next tide begins to rise that the West will have gained some right knowledge of the true philosophy of Man and Nature, and be then ready to bear the lifting of the veil a little more. To help on the progress of the race in this direction is the object of this book, and with that it is submitted to its readers in every part of the world.

CHAPTER XVII

INDEX

Abraham, an adept, 9-10
Absolute, word used for 'Space,' 15-16; no great teacher ascribes qualities to the, 16; no beginning or end to periods of manifestation in the, 17
Accident, after-death state of persons killed by, 122
Act, man reaps result of every, 102-3; no, performed without a thought, 103
Adam, meaning of story of, 144
Adepts, term for elder brothers, 7; Abraham, Moses, and Solomon, 9; scores of, in Indian literature, 11; may reach those in devachan, 130; may disperse and reunite atoms, 155; precipitate objects, 155-6; communicate across continents, 157
Akasa (Ākāśa), no English term for, 16; is produced from Matter and Spirit, 16
Alchemists, Nature's method known to, 145
America, historical and ethnological treasures of Central and South, burned by Spaniards, 10; sixth race to be evolved on, 29; new race being formed in, 135; zodiac of ancient, 138; ancient civilization in, 153
American, why ancient, races died out, 108
Animal(s), stage of monads in, kingdom, 30; has an ethereal double, 44; difference between man and, 61; extinct, forms will return to earth, 136; members of, kingdom cannot enter human kingdom, 146; evolved in prior chain of globes, 148; how differentiation of, began, 148-9
Annihilation, fate of those who choose left path, 67
Anthropology, esoteric, 147
Apes, origin of, 147; will die out, 146
Apollonius of Tyana, 9

Apparitions, explained, 48-9, 162-3
Apportation, 13-14, 49, 154-5, 158-9
Architect of universe, 14
Architecture, elder brothers preserve records of, 4
Arnold, Sir Edwin (quotation), 102
Art, elder brothers preserve records of, 4
Arthur, King, 135
Aryan Race, preserves doctrines, 96; now in kali yuga, 111
"As above, so below," 15
Astral Body, explanation of, 41-50; called linga sarira, 42; many names for, 43; composition of, 44; guiding model for physical body, 44-6; projection of, 46-7; contains true sense organs, 47, 50; appearance of, explained, 47-8, 168-9; state of, after death, 47; in conjunction with kama forms kama-rupa, 53; manas uses, to impress ideas, 63; dissipation of, 73; detaches from physical at death, 113; possibility of seeing, 162-4; adept may use, 163; of medium is loosely attached, 167; of medium used for materializations, 168; at death left in astral light, 170; of medium may be extended, 171; in distant years will act without physical body, 171
Astral Light, all forms exist in, 156; abuse of laws pertaining to, 158; pictures of past and future in, 160, 164; clairvoyant may read pictures in, 160-1; permeates the globe and atmosphere around it, 170; elemental beings in, 170
Atlanteans, renewed sin of the "Mindless," 147
Atma (Ātman), 7, 34-6; ray from Absolute Being, 60; and buddhi compose monad, 60; Higher Self, 65
Atma-buddhi-manas, the real man, 38; functions in devachan, 113, 123
Atom, germ of self-consciousness in every, 70; no, devoid of intelligence, 98; every, has memory, 117
Atoms, adept can control, 155
Attraction, and repulsion, 154
Aura, 169
Avatar (Avatāra), the, -cycle, 135; another great, yet to come, 135

Avichi (Avīchi), 120
Aztec Race, 108

Babylon, 96
Bach, descendants of, 83-4, 98
Bee, why, builds on geometrical rules, 98; produced and finished in preceding chain, 150-1
Bhagavad-Gītā, 8
Bhuta (Bhūta), 43, 165
Bible, 1, 20, 21, 137, 145
Birth, self sees causes for, 131
Birth-marks, origin of, 46
Black Magicians, 120-1
Blavatsky, H. P., agent of Great Lodge, 11-12, 44-5
Blind Tom, 97
Blood, one-way flow, 78
Body (see Physical Body; Rupa)
Boehme, Jacob, agent of the Great Lodge, 11-12
Brahma (Brahmā), life of, represents universe and worlds, 20; Life of, Day and Night of, 141-2
Brahmanda (Brahmānda), 141
Brahmanical (Brāhmanical), records, 19; cycles, 140-2
Brain, connection with mind, 59-61, 162-3; and lower manas, 63-4; convolutions of, caused by manas, 65; instrument for memory of soul, 86; renewed in each life, 86; reviews events of life at death, 112-13; generator of force, 155
British Isles, possible cataclysm to, 140
Buddha, taught ethics centuries before Jesus, 11; higher manas operative in a, 64-5; the last great avatar, 135
Buddhi, spiritual soul, 34, 36; spiritual discernment, 60; and atma, compose monad, 60; united with manas called Divine Ego, 65

Cagliostro, agent of Great Lodge, 11-12
Cain, story of, 144; other races existed before, 145

Capital Punishment, cause of many crimes, 54
Cataclysms, periodic, 17; four classes of, 139
Cell, composition of, 41
Cetus, and Jonah, 137-8
Character, national, 90-1; of persons, 104
Charlemagne, 135
Child, development of, in womb, 45; born deformed, 46, 103-4
China, 11, 87, 96
Chinese, believe in reincarnation, 71; were a nation of astronomers, 140
Christian Era, 34, 140
Christianity, a Jewish religion, 73; reincarnation in, 72-3
Chronology, Hindu, 21 (see Yuga)
Civilization, present, 57; cyclic streams of, 134, 137
Clairaudience, 41, 50, 161
Clairvoyance, 41, 50, 160-1
Clovis of France, 135
"Coats of Skin," explanation of verse in *Genesis*, 45
Cohesion, law of, 154-5
Color, mysteries of, 5
Communication, from an actual spirit is very rare, 55; possible immediately after death, 117-18; between adepts, 157; with the dead, 166-8
Confucius, 11, 65
Constellations, sun through zodiacal, 137-8
Constitution of Man, and planetary chain of globes, 33-4; sevenfold and threefold classification of, 34-5
Cosmos, occult, is behind visible phenomena, 163
Crime, capital punishment a cause of, 54; and sensitives, 122
Criminal, after-death state of executed, 122
Crucifixion, real meaning of, 75
Cycles, elder brothers know meaning of, 4; law of, 6-7; doctrine of, 132-43; Karma and Reincarnation interwoven with, 134; of avatars, 135; dynamic effects follow intersection of, 135-6; metonic and solar, 136; sidereal, 136; zodiacal, 137; cataclysms at

beginning and end of, 139; table of Brahmanical, 142; yugas and, 142; complete figures not given, 143

Day of Brahma, length of, 142
Death, caused by excess of life, 39-40; length of stay after, 88; state of man after, 94; every act registered at, 112; separation of man's principles at, 113-22; real man may communicate immediately after, 117-18; state of suicides and those killed by accident after, 121-2; last thoughts at, color devachan, 128
De Lesseps, 106
Desire(s), and passions of man, 51-4, 56-7, 115; cause of man's rebirth, 52, 74; cause of manifestation of worlds, 52; "Behind Will stands," 52; most developed in present evolution, 64; relation of, to skandhas, 115 (see Kama)
'Destroyers,' a class of 'lives,' 39
Devachan, heaven, 74; after death man's higher principles enter, 112-14, 123, 170; skandhas and, 116; kama loka is prelude to, 122; meaning of, 123; length of stay in, 123-8; vesture of ego in, 125, 129; last moment of life colors, 128; Mahatma K. H. on, 129; those in, cannot be reached except by adepts, 130-1
Devil, of Hindus is the Kama-rupa, 54
Dhyanis (Dhyānis), creators, aid evolution, 149
Differentiation, spirit is first, 16; of species, 148-9, 150-1
Dissolution, 29
Divine Ego, manas united with buddhi, 65
Dreams, argument for inner person's existence, 162
Drowning, review of lifetime during, 126
Dvapara Yuga (Dvāpara-yuga), length of, 142

Earth, inhabitants of, came from older world, 3; connected with other planets of solar system, 15; -chain, a sevenfold entity, 24; floats in an ocean of Life, 42; matter of, constantly evolving, 69-70; population of, 86-8; reimbodiment on, 89, 94; kama loka and, 113; astral matter of, 114; life on, is a kama loka, 116-17; solidification of, 133; surface of, changed when poles shifted, 136;

material of, affected by man, 136; enters new spaces at completion of sidereal cycle, 136-7; cataclysms, 136, 139-40; evolution of, proceeds under Manu, 141; three hundred million years in astral stage, 150

Earth Chain, seven globes of, constitute one great globe, 26; reimbodiment of former chain, 26-7; number of egos limited on, 27 (see Planetary Chain)

Earthquakes, 139

Edom, kings of, 19-20

Ego, 23; reincarnation of, 76-8; and heredity, 82-3; length of post-mortem states varies, 88, 126; in devachan, 130-1

Egos, number of, limited on Earth Chain, 27

Egypt, intercourse between India and, 19; reason for loss of civilization of, 96; Denderah Zodiac of, 138

Egyptians, king-initiates of, members of the Great Lodge, 8; no living school of ancient learning of, 18; Jews preserved part of learning of, 19; reincarnating in America, 19; descendants of, 83; karma of the, 109; and American nation, 109; cycles of, derived from Indian sages, 140

Elder Brothers, activity and work of, 3-7, 14; are perfected men, 6-7; known by various names, 7 (see Masters)

Electricity, 139-40, 170

Elementals, 5, 118-19; aid mediums, 159; exist in astral light, 170

Elementary(ies), 43

Elias, reincarnated as John the Baptist, 72

Embryology, mysteries of, 44-6

English Language, lacks philosophical terms, 43, 59-60

Esoteric Buddhism, mistaken conceptions of, 25-6; calls evolving stream of monads "life wave," 27-8; classification of man's principles, 34; written from suggestions of adepts, 34, 51, 126; length of stay in devachan, 126

Ethereal Body, 44-5

Ethics, truth concerning, preserved in India, 10; taught by Buddha and Jesus and Confucius, 11; reason for, 109; must precede psychic development, 172

Eve, hidden truth in story of, 144
Evolution, theosophical conception of, 24; hastened by manas, 66; object of, 68-9; double, 69; devachan a necessity for, 124; dhyanis aid, 149; midway point of, 149

Fakir, uses natural forces for producing phenomena, 153-4, 159
Family Karma, 106
Fatalism, karma is not, 102
Fires, universal, 140
Flood, story of, in many nations, 17; origin of belief in, 29-30; cause of, 139-40
Fossils, 151
Fourth Principle, of man, 51-8; desires and passions originate in, 51-3, 56; balance principle, 52-3
Frederic III of Germany, 135
Free Masons, allegory of Solomon's Temple, 21-2
Fruits, from former planet, 148

Gases, 37-8, 139
Genius, explanation of, 97
Ghost, 49
God, 21; man will evolve into a, 68-9, 75
Godhood, the goal of evolution, 68
Gods, have not bodies like humans, 123
Globe(s), planetary chain constitutes one great, 26; visible, are fourth-plane, 27; seven rounds on, 28
Gravitation, 154
Great Breath, 17
Great Lodge (see Lodge)
Greek Hymn, used by early Christian Fathers, 90
Greeks, taught reincarnation, 71; cycles of, derived from India, 140

Happiness, and unhappiness, 109
Heavenly Man, Jewish teaching about, 75; man ever reaching towards, 144

Heredity, and reincarnation, 82-4; does not affect real ego, 82-3; not the cause of essential nature, 91; not the cause of genius, 97-8
Higher Manas, and genius, 64; operative in sages, 64-5; shells devoid of, 120-1
Higher Self, Atma may be called, 65
Hindus, 6-7; preserve old ideas, 19; did not admit creation out of nothing, 21
Hindustan, records of, 19
Horses, root-type of, 150
Human, development of present form of, 45; extinct, forms will return to earth, 136 (see Man)
Human Beings, on one round, appear before animals, 30
Human Kingdom, lower kingdoms cannot enter in this cycle, 30, 146
Humanity, eighteen million years old, 31
Huxley, T. H., 2
Hypnotism, 13, 63, 103; improper experiments in, 172-3

Ice Cataclysms, cause of, 140
Ideas, inherent, implanted by elder brothers, 98
Idiocy, not due to heredity, 98
Imagination, 52-3, 156
Impressions, produce pictures in aura of man, 169
India, people of, preservers of philosophical truths, 10-11; early intercourse between Egypt and, 19; reason for isolation of, 140-1
Indian (American), mistreatment of, will be adjusted by karma, 109
Individuality, and manas, 65; raises all matter in earth chain, 66
Inner Ego, 65
Inner God, 56, 58
Inner Senses, not hindered by trance or sleep, 169 (see Senses)
Insanity, 64
Instinct, 97-8
Intellect, without buddhi and atma is selfish, 62

Intelligence, not present when connection between manas and brain is broken, 62-3
Intelligences governing nature were once human, 2
Intuition, does not depend on reason, 61-2

Jesus, ethics of, also taught by Buddha, 11; higher manas operative in, 65; taught reincarnation, 71; what, meant by resurrection, 74; an avatar of the Jews, 135
Jews, preserved part of learning of Egyptians, 19; hidden meaning of scriptures, 19; believed in reincarnation, 71-2; fated to wander, 109
Jiva (Jīva), life energy, 39; prana and, 42
Job (33:15-16), on dreams and visions, 162
John the Baptist, reincarnation of Elias, 71-2
John the Revelator, on reincarnation (*Rev.*, 3:12), 72
Jonah, and the Whale, 137
Judgment Day, meaning of, 29-30
Justice, in nature, 84; human, imperfect, 85

Kali Yuga, black age, 141; length of, 142; commenced at Krishna's death, 142
Kalpa, "cycle," 132; length of, 142
Kama (Kāma), "desire," 51; fourth principle of man, 51-8; in conjunction with astral body forms Kama-rupa, 53; and after-death state, 115; relation of skandhas to, 115-16
Kama Loka (Kāma-loka), 112-22; man's principles enter, at death, 112-14; penetrates and surrounds earth, 113; infinitely varied, 114; desires and thoughts exist in, 116; state of man in, 117; suicides and victims of accident, 121-2; prelude to devachan, 122
Kama-rupa (Kāma-rūpa), 34, 51-8; incites crimes, 54; made up of astral body and passions, 113; in Kama loka, 117
Karma, 72-90; doctrine of, 100-11; inextricably interlaced with reincarnation, 100, 134; the law of ethical causation, 100; explains misery in world, 101-2, 108-9; beneficent and just, 102; three classes of, 104-6; national and racial, 107-9; *The Secret Doctrine*

on, 110-11; acts on beings in devachan, 123 (see Reincarnation and Cycles)
Kingdoms of Nature, first outlined in ideal form, 45; purpose of evolution of, 69-70; evolution of, aided by dhyanis, 149; vast period of time passed by, in astral stage, 150
King-Initiates, in ancient Egypt, 8
Krishna, Hindu avatar, 135
Krita Yuga (Kṛita-Yuga), "Golden Age," 141-2

Languages, dead, will reappear, 136
Lévi, Eliphas, 35
Levitation, 154
Life, 17, 42-3; universally pervasive, 42; objections to one-life theory, 93-4; earth-, is a kama loka, 116-17; thirst for, lodged in skandhas, 127; of soul is endless, 128
Life Energy, prana or jiva, 39; absorbed during sleep, 40; returns to its source at death of body, 42
Life Principle, 45
Life Wave, evolutionary process of, 27-8
Light, and darkness, 6
Light of Asia, The (quotation), 102
Limbs, why amputated, are still felt, 46
Linga-Sarira (Linga-śarīra), 34, 41-4 (see Astral Body)
Lodge, Egyptian rulers members of Great, 8; agents of the Great, enumerated, 11-12; hopes of the, 173 (see Masters)
Lokas, 113
Longfellow, 65
Love, 130
Lower Manas, four peculiarities of, 64; result of misuse, 121

Mahatma, "great soul," 7; term used in northern India, 8; in *Bhagavad-Gītā*, 8; has power over space, time, and mind, 13; may help entities in devachan, 130-1
Maha Yuga (Mahā-yuga), comprises four yugas, 142
Mammals, produced in fourth round, 147

Man, on systems of globes prior to solar system, 2-3; watched over by elder brothers, 3; production of perfect, 7; has germ of powers of mahatma, 13, 14; over 18 million years old, 23; evolution from ethereal to physical, 23; seven-fold constitution of, 24, 32-7; correspondence of, with seven globes, 25-6; threefold division of, 32-3; length of life of, 37; inner powers of, 49-50; development of mind, 56, 60-2; a quaternary, 57; difference between animal and, 61; senses in, 62-3; permanent individuality of, 65-6; goal of, 66; inner body of, made of thought, 67; purpose of evolution of, 68-9; cannot go back to animal kingdom, 76-7; never loses his identity, 92; maker of his own destiny, 102; state of, after death, 112-31; astral, in kama loka, 117; four classes of shells of, after death, 119-21; extinct forms of, will return to earth, 136; cycles and, 136-7; knowledge given to, by sages, 138-9; will ever exist, 144; seven races of, appeared simultaneously, 144; evolution of, during seven rounds, 144-5; prior to earth chain evolved on Lunar chain, 146-47; relation of anthropoids to, 147; had a gigantic ape-like form in third and fourth round, 147; astral prototypes, 150; highest product of evolution, 153

Manas, 34-6, 59-67; inner god and, 56; man's fifth principle, 59-60; enlightenment of, 60-1; needs enlightenment of buddhi and atma, 62, 65; lower, four peculiarities of, 64; deluded by desire, 66-7; bound by magnetic threads to earth, 67; not fully active, 64-5, 67; the thinker, cannot return to baser forms, 76-8; nature of, requires devachan, 124; knowledge gained by soul stored in, 134-5; light of, not in third race, but in fourth, 148; necessary aid in evolution, 149

Manifestation, periods of, known by ancients, 6-7; object of, 7; no beginning or end of periods of, 16-17

Manu, evolution of globe proceeds under, 141; length of, 142

Manu (*Laws of Manu*), teachings on transmigration, 76-7

Manvantara, "between two Manus," 141; length of, 142

Mars, a fourth plane globe, 27

Masters, on their work, 5-6; term used by H. P. B. for mahatmas, 7; on devachan, 127, 129; on anthropoids, 147; on differentiation

in nature, 151; man highest product of evolution, 153 (see Elder Brothers)
Materialist, devachan of, 127
Materializations, explanations of, at séances, 47-8, 53-4, 118; process of, 168
Matter, definition of, 16; primordial, equivalent for mulaprakriti, 16; constantly in motion, 41, 50; of this globe has been through every kind of form, 66, 69-70; purpose of evolution of, 68-70; constantly undergoing change, 139; indestructible under organic rather than inorganic forms, 151; is held suspended in the air, 156
Meditation, stream of life's, stored in manas, 62
Medium, materializations by, 47-8, 53-6, 118-19; four classes of shells visit the, 119-21; cannot help those in devachan, 130; a pure, may rarely commune with egos in devachan, 131, 166; explanation of apportation produced by, 159; practices of, constitute necromancy, 165; loosely attached astral body of, 167; generally come to grief, 168; astral body of, used for producing materializations, 168; astral body of, may be extended, 171 ; at the mercy of shells in kama loka, 172
Mediumship, dangers of, 171-2
Memory, connection of, with Lower Manas, 63-4; objections as to loss of, of former lives answered, 84-6; is preserved in inner man, 86; many have, of prior lives, 86; preceding, blotted out in devachan, 131
Menes, Egyptian avatar, 135
Mental Planes, karma works on, 104-5, 106-7
Mercury, a fourth-plane globe, 27
Mesmer, an agent of the Great Lodge, 11; taught hypnotism under another name, 12
Metempsychosis, applies to whole cosmos, 71
Metonic Cycle, a period of nineteen years, 136
Mind, the intelligent part of cosmos, 16; universal, 16-17; of man evolving, 57; explanation of, 59-67; given to man by evolved beings, 60-1; entity in devachan functions on plane of, 125; brain and, can evolve forms, 163 (see Manas)

Mind-reading, 13, 41; by adept, 157-8; abuse of power of, 158
"Mindless," evolution of, men, 60-1; the sin of the, 147
Mineral, stage of monads in, kingdom, 30; has an ethereal double, 44; matter composing, will evolve to human matter, 70
Missing Links, science unable to find, 151
Mohammed, a minor intermediate avatar, 135
Monad, composed of atma and buddhi, 60
Monads, now evolving on earth came from moon, 27; evolving stream of, termed life wave, 27-8; evolutionary process of, described, 27-9; no more, emerge into human stage after middle of fourth round, 30; begin work in elemental conditions, 30
Moon, the fourth globe of moon chain, 27; on same plane of perception as earth, 27; cycle of the, 136; motion of, 141-2; races of men evolved on the, chain, 146, 148; lower kingdoms evolved on, 148
Moon Chain, seven energy centers of, evolve on earth chain, 26-8; stream of egos from, had arrived before middle of fourth round, 27
Moses, an adept, 9-10; a great influence on nations, 135
Mozart, genius proves previous lives, 97
Mulaprakṛiti (Mūlaprakṛiti), "primordial matter," 16
Murder, after-death state of persons killed by, 121-2; executed criminals incite sensitives to commit crime, 122
Mysteries of Greece, 6-7

Napoleon, 97, 106; reincarnation of Charlemagne, 97, 135
Nations, reason for differences between, 90-1; rise and decay of, 95-6; cycles of, 134, 137
Nature, is sentient, 2; exists for the soul's experience, 2; laws of, unalterable, 79-80, 84-5; laws of, demonstrate effects follow causes, 89; karma is the most important law of, 100; is always kind, 129; never works in haste, 145, 151; final goal of, 151
Necromancy, prohibited by Roman Catholic Church, 153; prohibited by spiritual teachers, 165
Night of Brahma, length of, 142

Nitya Pralaya, continual change and destruction, 40-1
Noah, 10; meaning of story of, 144

Paracelsus, an agent of the Great Lodge, 11; originated valuable methods in medicine, 12
Parsees, 61
Passions, and desires of man, 51-4, 56-7, 115-16; cause of man's rebirth, 52, 74; two aspects of, 53; relation to skandhas, 115-16
Path, man must make conscious choice of his, 67; left, leads to annihilation, 67
Path, The, 129, 141
Paul, teaches threefold nature of man, 32; taught preexistence, 72; on resurrection, 74; taught karma, 102
Phenomena, requirements for production of, 154-60; factors for understanding of psychic, 169-71
Philosophy, elder brothers preserve records of, 4; cyclic appearance of true, 6, 14; and ethics must be learned before development of powers, 172
Physical Body, explanation of, 26, 34-8; constituents of, 39-41; built up of "lives," 39; undergoes complete change every seven years, 40-1; alters every moment, 44; astral body is model for, 44; man's passions and desires not due to, 51; does not reincarnate, 73; operation of karma on, 106-7; resolved into nature at death, 113; violent loss of, is not real death of man, 122; necessity for death of, 129
Planetary Chain, sevenfold, intimately connected with man's evolution, 24; globes of, are in coadunation but not in consubstantiality, 26; clue to doctrine of, 33-4
Planets, visible, are fourth plane globes, 27
Polarity, change of, accomplishes levitation, 154
Poles, shifting of, on earth, 136, 140
Population, objections regarding, and reincarnation, 86-8; egos composing world's, constitute a definite number, 86-8
Prana (Prāṇa), "vitality," 34; life energy, 39; meaning of, 42; jiva and, 42; astral body is vehicle of, 42-3

Precipitation, explanation of, 14, 155-6
Preservers, class of "lives," 39-40
Principles of Man, sevenfold classification, 15, 34; related to seven cosmic principles, 24; separation of, after death, 113; cohesive force of, 121
Prodigies, 97
Psychic Energies, stored in manas, 124
Psychic Phenomena, enumeration of factors for understanding of, 169-71
Psychic Powers, danger of selfish use of, 172; philosophy and ethics must be practised before development of, 172-3
Psychology, western, 51; true, lacking in West, 152; true, belongs to the Orient, 153
Purgatory, kama loka origin of Christian theory, 113-14
Pyramid of Gizeh, 18-19

Quaternary, Lower, classification of, 36-8; man is fully developed in, 57

Race(s), definition of term, 28-9; sixth, to be evolved on Americas, 29; reason for the extinction, 95-6; inherent ideas implanted in, by the elder brothers, 98; cycles of the, 134-7; affects material of globe, 136; yugas do not affect all, at same time, 141; evolution divided into four yugas for every, 141; seven, appeared simultaneously, 144-5; evolution of, on Lunar Chain, 146; at close of third, man had an ape-like form, 147; unnatural unions occurred in third, 147
Rajas, quality of activity, 56; gives impulse to evolution, 56
Rama (Rāma), Hindu avatar, 135
Reason, lower aspect of manas, 61-2
Rebirth, desire causes, 52, 67; a necessity until causes eliminated, 91 (see Reincarnation)
Reembodiment, doctrine of, 69-70 (see Reincarnation)
Reincarnation, doctrine of, 69-78, 79-88, 89-99; applies to whole cosmos and not to man alone, 69-71; ancients believed in, 71;

doctrine of, in Bible, 71-3; taught by Church until debarred by Council, 72, 79; "the lost chord of Christianity," 73; does not mean transmigration into animals, 76-8; objections to, answered, 79-88, 89-99; law of, interwoven with Karma and Cycles, 134
Reincarnation, by Annie Besant, 87
Religion, elder brothers preserve records of, 4; results of conflict between science and, 59
Repulsion, attraction and, 154
Rest, periods of manifestation and of, 7; period of, takes place between races, 29
Roman Catholic Church, has always admitted psychic world, 153; prohibited necromancy, 153; phenomena produced by saints of, 154
Root-types, missing link between astral, and fossils undiscovered by science, 151
Round, definition of term, 28; no egos entered earth after fourth, 28; seven races came simultaneously in first, 144; seven races are amalgamated in second, 145; seven races will be distinct in seventh, 145; man had a gigantic ape-like form in third, 147; mammals were produced in fourth, 147
Row, Subba, on classification of man, 35
Rupa (Rūpa), "body," 34

Sages, in India born with complete knowledge of philosophy, 97
Saint-Germain, an agent of the Great Lodge, 11
Saint-Martin, Count, an agent of the Great Lodge, 11-12
Satya Yuga, age of purity, 111; golden age, 141; length of, 142
Savage(s), 92, 95-6
Science, results of conflict between religion and, 59; theosophy differs with, as to origin of man, 144; cannot find missing links, 151; necessity for, to admit of astral and inner senses, 151
Séances, phenomena at, 47-9, 53-6, 118, 119; four classes of shells present at, 119-21; explanation of materializations at, 168
Second Sight, 161

Secret Doctrine, The, on seven globes, 26; on reason for withdrawing teachings, 33-4; on karma, 110-11; on man and apes, 147
Seed, produces its own kind because of ethereal double, 44
Self, sees causes that led it to devachan and back just before birth, 131
Self-consciousness, the final aim of evolution is, 68; every part of nature has the possibility of, 68-9
Senses, first exist in germ, 23; become concentrated to actual, on astral plane, 23-4; pertain to astral body, 38; real seat of man's, are in astral body, 50; manas necessary for functioning of, 62-3; three modes of functioning of, 164; inner, necessary for perceiving occult cosmos, 163; inner, not hindered by trance or sleep, 169
Seth, 144
Seven Principles, reason for classification of, 15; man's, related to cosmic, 24; enumeration of, 34
Seventh Race, dissolution comes after full perfection of, 29
Sexes, shape of man before appearance of, 23, 31; did not exist ages ago, 23
Shakespeare, 84
"Shell" of Man, condition of, in kama loka, 117-18; contains automatic consciousness, 117; four classes of, 119-21; astral, may produce apparitions, 162
Sidereal Year, length of, 136; brings earth into newer spaces, 137
Sight, faculty of, 62-3; three modes of, 164 (see Vision)
Sinnett, A. P., extract from Master's letter published by, 5-6; mistaken conceptions of, 26; sevenfold classification of man of, 34; author of *Esoteric Buddhism,* 126
Sixth Race, to be evolved on Americas, 29
Skandhas, the aggregates that make up man, 115-16; relation of, to kama; 115-16; are being made daily, 116; combine at rebirth to form new set, 116; thirst for life is lodged in, 127
Sleep, restores equilibrium, 40; state of lower manas during, 64; inner man may commune with higher intelligences during, 162; does not hinder inner senses from acting, 169

Smyth, Piazzi, and Pyramid of Gizeh, 18
Solar System, man and mind existed before, condensed, 3, 60; is conscious on every plane, 103; end of, 133
Solomon, an adept, 9-10; no trace found of temple of, 19; allegory of, 21-2; on reincarnation (*Proverbs* 8:22), 72
Sons of the Sun, in ancient Egypt, 8
Sons of Wisdom, the elder brothers of men on any globe, 61; enlightened manas in men, 61
Soul, Christian teachings concerning, 32-3; immortal and parentless, 81; Church teaches each, is a new creation, 89; early Christian Fathers taught, fell into matter, 90
Soulless Men, live in astral sphere, 170-1
Sound, mysteries of, known to elder brothers, 5; a distinguishing characteristic of astral sphere, 159; every, produces an image, 160
Space, 16
Species, reason for differentiation of, 150-1
Spencer, Herbert, theory of, 21
Spirit, the first differentiation is, 16; akasa is produced from matter and, 16-17; will is the force of, in action, 16
Spirits, explanation of so-called return of, 47-50, 53-6
Spiritual Soul, buddhi may be called man's, 65
Spiritualism(ist), 47-50, 53-6; called so wrongly, 152, 165; has no philosophy, 152; practices of, constitute necromancy, 165; modern cult of, originated in Rochester, 165; seven objections, theories, 167-8
Spook, at séances, 47-50, 53-6; kama-rupa, is enemy of civilization, 54
Sub-races, why, are evolved, 29
Suffering, and reincarnation, 84, 94, 108; dogma of eternal, 130
Suicides, state of, in kama loka, 121-2; are not really dead, 121; must remain in kama loka until natural life term is reached, 122
Sun, cycle of the, 136
Swedenborg, 50

Talleyrand, Prince, Memoirs of, state Napoleon said he was Charlemagne, 97
Tamas, quality of darkness and indifference, 56; dominion of, ends with annihilation, 56
Tanha (Taṇhā), "thirst for life," 127
Telepathy, shows existence of other planes of consciousness, 13; physical explanation of, 41
Tennyson, 65
Theosophy, definition of, 1-2; not formulated or invented by man, 1; differs from science as to origin of man, 144
Thought, sum-total of man's, stored in manas, 61-4; every, makes a physical and mental link with a desire, 67; man's inner body made of, 67; root of every act, 103; karma stored in, may act in future life, 105; last stream of, governs man's after-death state, 114-15, 128; every, combines with an elemental, 116; inseparably connected with their evolver, 116; mass of, exists in kama loka, 116
Time, regarding earth and solar system, 125; no, in devachan, 125-6
Trance, inner senses not hindered from acting during, 169
Transformation, of matter, 69-70
Transition Period, present age is a, 4, 57, 143
Transmigration, does not mean reincarnation, 76-8; explanation of teaching on, 76-8
Treta Yuga (Tretā-yuga), length of, 142
Triad, Higher, classification of, 36; goes to another state at death, 47; only partly developed in man, 57; the immortal pilgrim, 59, 74; enters devachan after death, 74; does not fully reincarnate, 75; begins to function after death, 113

Unhappiness, 109
Universe, evolves from Unknown on seven planes, 15; sevenfold division of, enumerated, 15; theosophical view of purpose of, 68-9; is under the sway of karma, 100
Universal Mind, plan for evolution comes first in, 30

Vegetable, stage of monads in, kingdom, 30; has ethereal double, 44; present, matter will evolve to animal matter, 70

Venus, habitation of more progressed entities than earth, 3; a fourth-plane globe, 27
Vibration, rates of, determine the different cycles, 133
Virchow, Professor, in regard to missing link, 151
Vishnu Purana (*Vishṇu-Purāṇa*), Wilson's translation of, 21
Vision, faculty of, 62-3; spiritual, very rare among clairvoyants, 161; how spiritual, may be developed, 161; prophetic, possible during sleep, 162; three modes of, 164
Vow, made through will and desire, 52

Waking, state of, resists life energy, 40
Washington, George, 135
Water, 37-8; cause of displacement of, on earth, 139-40
West, materialistic civilization in, 12; present age in the, is kali-yuga, 141; liberty of thought is present in the, 142
Wheat, origin on another globe chain, 151
Will, force of spirit in action, 16; "Behind, stands desire," 52; is all powerful, 156; results of use of, and imagination, 156-7
Wilson, calls Hindu chronology fiction, 21
"Word made flesh," 75
World(s), all, have septenary constitution, 15; plan for evolution of, in Universal Mind, 16; end of, recorded in tradition as a cataclysm, 17; age of, known to Orientals, 18; Mosaic account of genesis of, imposed on the West, 18; what causes the end of the, 29

Yogee (Yogī or Yogin), Hindu, can make distant objects approach, 49; uses natural forces for producing phenomena, 153-4
Yuga(s), major and minor, must be accomplished, 6; nearest Sanskrit word to "cycle," 132; explanation of and length of the four, 141-2

Zodiac, symbology of, 137-8; Denderah, 138
Zoroaster, 65; Persian avatar, 135

Eddie Garza
5602 Ludington Dr.
Houston, TX 77035